spymom

val agosta
with dee axelrod
afterword by Christine Agosta Quintana

Guideposts
New York, New York

Spymom

ISBN: 978-0-8249-4777-4

Published by Guideposts
16 East 34th Street
New York, New York 10016
www.guideposts.com

Distributed by Ideals Publications, a division of Guideposts
2636 Elm Hill Pike, Suite 120
Nashville, Tennessee 37214

Guideposts and *Ideals* are registered trademarks of Guideposts.

Acknowledgments

Every attempt has been made to credit the sources of copyrighted material used in this book. If any such acknowledgment has been inadvertently omitted or miscredited, receipt of such information would be appreciated.

Library of Congress Cataloging-in-Publication Data

Agosta, Val.
    Spymom / by Val Agosta with Dee Axelrod.
        p. cm.
    ISBN 978-0-8249-4777-4
    1. Agosta, Val. 2. Women private investigators—Idaho—Boise—Biography.
    I. Axelrod, Dee. II. Title. III. Title: Spy mom.
    HV8083.A55A3 2010
    363.28'9092—dc22
    [B]

                                    2009042531r

Cover design by Mingovits Design
Cover illustration by Jonathan Carlson
Interior design by Lorie Pagnozzi
Typeset by Nancy Tardi

Printed and bound in the United States of America
10 9 8 7 6 5 4 3 2 1

Author's Note

ALL OF THE CHARACTERS AND EVENTS IN THIS BOOK ARE REAL, though some names and details have been changed to protect the innocent and the guilty. On occasion, characters and timelines have been conflated, and the boring parts have been taken out, but my intention has been to stay true to the people and events involved.

Prologue
Close Pursuit

IT'S PITCH BLACK IN THE ALLEY.

The streetlight is defunct, and the chill October night, moonless.

I kill the headlights as we turn down the passageway behind the rows of run-down houses. In the absolute dark, the crunch of gravel under the tires sounds extra loud. I feel the tall, saw-toothed fences pressing close. We stop behind the only house with an unenclosed yard.

"Your turn, Mollie," I say.

"I'm on it." She's out of the car before it stops rolling.

Mollie doesn't want to look at what we know is in that house any more than I do, but she raises the binoculars to check for movement. I think, for perhaps the thousandth time, how lucky I have been in my partners. First Jan and now Mollie. Two for two.

"No one," she says.

I've been to this house before. A self-proclaimed psychic, the owner once made a bid to offer her psychic powers to my PI firm, Hanady Investigations. When that didn't pan out, she tried to hire us to locate an old girlfriend. We declined. We didn't know until later that she had planned to kill her former lover once we found her.

Now the tables are turned. We've been hired to investigate this woman we'd come so close to signing as a client. They're dealers—she and her posse of supersized friends. We're here to take her trash, hoping to find drug paraphernalia to prove her guilt.

Mollie absolutely loves to go through trash. Trash holds a wealth of personal data and can usually be had for minimal risk. For her, a trash can is a treasure trove, and she explores with the guilty pleasure of the true addict. My bag of cast-off belongings is Mollie's bag of hidden possibilities. She pokes happily through moldy potato peelings and wadded tissues, because, according to her, you never know when you might find the combination to the safe or the skeleton head. She spends hours reconstructing shredded documents like some people do jigsaw puzzles.

Tonight, she pulls on latex gloves.

"Go for it, girl," I say. "I'm right behind you."

I hang back, though, letting her get a good head start before I trade the warm truck for the cold alley. The nip in the air is a preview of the Boise winter closing fast. Also, I don't want to spill garbage on my favorite T-shirt—a gift from my daughter—which says "Private Eyes Are Watching YOU" in curlicue cursive. We might be middle-aged moms with seven kids between us, but we can still dress up and look good. Mollie, who is blonde and slight and—at forty-four—six years younger than I am, can look really spectacular.

Tonight, though, she's all business as she flings back the lid of the dumpster. I hear the clank of empty bottles as she piles trash bags in the back of my Silverado. We're almost there, almost home, when a car slowly rolls into view at the end of the alley and pauses. I back the darkened truck toward Mollie. *Maybe they can't make us out. Maybe I can quietly roll out the other end, headlights off.*

The car slams into reverse and whips into the alley. "They're after us," I yell to Mollie. "Get in! We're out of here!"

I'm rolling backward as she flings herself into the passenger seat. The intensifying glare from onrushing headlights spotlights Mollie's white face, her widening eyes. She mouths the words *dang, dang, dang.*

I back into a driveway and turn around. The battered jeep is almost on us. I pull out just ahead of them, reflexively flipping on the headlights.

Mollie hisses at me, "Off, turn them *off.*" Mollie knows this part of town, so she navigates, pointing left and right. I zip down side streets, cut across church parking lots, turn into alleys, but I can't shake them. It's not like in the movies where they always lose the bad guys. You'd think their car was chained to my bumper. Then I realize they're trying to ram us.

"Left, there." Mollie points. I'm half a block down the street before the Dead End sign registers.

"Pull a u-ee, pull a u-eee," she's yelling in my ear. I make the U-turn and pass the car headed in the other direction.

I already know these women are dangerous. I know from our brief acquaintance that they slap and head-butt people as signs of affection. *If slamming someone's head is considered casual contact, what do you do when you're really mad?* I'm actually numb with terror, driving on autopilot.

"Get to a main street," Mollie says. "Get to where there are people."

I turn onto busy Broadway, headlights still off. They turn, too, and pull up beside us. We're neck and neck. We can see them shaking their fists. We can hear them screaming. When we stop at a red light, they careen into the oncoming traffic and turn across my car at a right angle, cutting us off. The car doors fly open and they advance on Mollie. I just have time to take in these women with giant breasts that whomp with every stride, kah-*boom*, bah-kah-*boom*.

I back up, while Mollie practically climbs out the car window to signal the cars behind us to wait. I pass the jeep on the left while Mollie yells, "Eat our dust!" We run the red, Dukes of Hazard on caffeine. We pass a blur of cars. I see flickering footage of white faces as we pass. Bystanders are talking into cell phones. They're calling the police.

Mollie grabs for her own phone.

"No," I say. "I can still lose them."

"They're after us, they want us, they're not going to stop," she says as she dials 911.

Mollie relays instructions to the operator, and I exit right, onto the freeway ramp, flashing my lights so the police will know it's us. Four squad cars sweep right in behind us—two black SUVs from each side —lights flashing, sirens blaring. They cut everyone off, and we sail down the empty freeway. I yell, "*Whoo-hoo*" and "Whoa mamma" while Mollie, head out the window, announces to the sky, "We are so cool. So. Un-be-lieve-ably. Cool."

When we get off the freeway and double back on local streets, like the 911 operator instructs, we see that see all traffic is at a standstill except for one lane. At the head of the jam is the turquoise jeep, already swarming with drug dogs and police. The handcuffed women are being stuffed into a squad car.

We pull up next to the squad cars, and a police officer tells us that they have outstanding warrants on these women that have nothing to do with us. In fact, the officer says, the women have no idea who we really are. They told police they thought we were DEA agents. They don't have any idea that we're the spymoms.

🝙

Another cop, a hunky twenty-something, walks over to where we're parked. I see his eyes flicker over the interior of my truck, taking in the soda cups, candy wrappers and charge slips—all the trash that accumulates in the spymobile that doubles as the family car.

Then we get the lecture we probably deserve. He lays into us about the danger of crossing the drug underworld and how this is not a game. It's not something for us to be involved with. We need to leave it for the police to do. What makes us think we can encounter meth dealers, he asks, and not get in trouble?

"Yes, sir." I nod. "Yes, sir." Mollie fishes around in her purse. I know what she's looking for, even before she pulls out a picture of Staci, her gorgeous and single daughter. She holds the photo out to show Officer Handsome.

The police, in general, have no great love for private investigators, let alone lady PIs. We're middle-aged, mommy PIs, so we're more than used to their condescending attitude. But tonight, we're willing to take it, because they really went to bat for us. They did their job, and they saved us.

Tonight we love them all.

By the time they let us go, it's midnight, but we are still too stoked with adrenaline to sleep. Your typical guy PI would head to the nearest bar to buy the boys a round. But we're spymoms. We drive to the nearest Albertson's, where we sip Cokes at the grocery store's closed Starbucks and high-five and laugh like maniacs. We relive the chase and ask each other, "How did you feel when . . . and *then* how did you feel?"

We marvel at our escape. We're at the top of our form, invincible as superheroes.

If I had known what lay ahead, I might not have been in such high spirits that night, but I didn't have any clue that soon I'd face danger that would make the car chase—the most dangerous caper since I opened my spy firm three years ago—seem like a lark. Somewhere down the dark alley of the future, an old enemy waits.

But for now, we celebrate into the small hours of the night, and eventually pack it in so we can face our husbands and kids in the morning. Even Superwoman sometimes has to empty the dishwasher.

Chapter 1

Nancy Drew

IT ALL STARTED WITH NANCY DREW.

She was the only friend who was there with me through my childhood. My father's service career had taken Mom and us kids—me, Vickie (born just eleven months before me), Henry and Jan—from Alaska to the Philippines, Libya, Washington State, New York State and many points in between. We must have moved a million times.

I was a shy kid, the kind of child who clings to her mother's skirts. I never went to the same school two years in a row, and that's not easy, even for the most outgoing kid. It helped somewhat that I went to military-run schools—which meant that everyone else was in transit too—but I still struggled.

The exception was our four-year stay on Elmendorf Air Force base in Anchorage, Alaska, from the fourth grade through the seventh—the happiest years of my childhood. The base we lived on was twenty-one square miles of near-wilderness just north of Anchorage. In winter, the dads had to take turns keeping watch at the schoolyard so we could have recess without sharing the playground with grizzly bears or moose.

In summer, though, the whole base was our playground. We'd run wild all day, and as long as we were home for dinner, all was well.

We lived in a tiny two-story military town house on the base. Each building had six town houses linked in a long row, with every two homes sharing the same front porch and back stairs.

My mother's sister and her family also lived on the base; having extended family with us—including Carol, a cousin—made me feel at home. In addition, I soon had two new friends. One was an adventuresome girl my own age and grade level, Ellie. The other was, of course, Nancy Drew.

I don't recall how I got my hands on that first Nancy Drew mystery. The base had a library, and Anchorage had bookstores. Books were also passed from hand to hand among the kids. However it happened, when I started that first Nancy Drew mystery, *The Secret of the Old Clock,* I was hooked. I read the whole series. Wrapped in a comforter on the sofa, I'd read straight through each new book from first page to last. I passed many dark winter days with her, solving mysteries together.

Nancy Drew was my literary big sister and role model. She was smart and independent. Young and beautiful, of course. She was an eighteen-year-old with unlimited freedom, a bottomless bank account and a brand-new blue convertible. She lived with her attorney father and a housekeeper, but she could come and go at will. She didn't attend school or hold a regular job, but she had a ready supply of cash. She was perfectly coifed, dressed and styled.

She was also amazingly accomplished. She had a race car driver's reflexes, could ride and shoot, and was a gourmet chef. She was at home on a tennis court or on the water. Swimming, sailing, slicing through the waves in a motorboat—it was all one to Nancy Drew. With just a little help from her dad, she solved every puzzle and uncovered every mystery.

I pictured finding the passageway behind the clock myself. I wanted to follow it and discover treasure. I knew that by finding the treasure, I would be able to help the orphan kids next door. I also wanted her convertible—not powder blue or baby blue, but something like cerulean, I was sure—and her boyfriend, Ned. Although I couldn't articulate this as a preteen, I envied her competence and her confident femininity.

Whatever uncertainty I felt about my own abilities or my place in the world beyond my family, whatever discomfort I felt about the changes stirring in my body, whatever confusion I had as the 1960s advanced and the world began to change, I knew I could count on adventure and safety in the pages of those books.

That Nancy Drew had inspired generations of girls since her debut in the 1930s meant nothing to me. I discovered each book as if I were the very first reader. I didn't so much compare myself to Nancy Drew as absorb her. We were one.

Once I started reading mysteries, I wanted to solve my own, so I founded a detective agency, and I developed a series of "cases" to work on. I called my detective agency Hanady Investigations. I made up the name Hanady. It had the right weight for the name of a grown-up business, I thought. I liked saying the word. I liked the way the three clipped syllables rolled off the tongue. Dad liked the name too. He said it sounded "steady but happy, energetic and full of vinegar," just like me.

Like Nancy Drew, I soon found that sleuthing gave me a link to my father. Although he was so busy establishing and maintaining communications for the Air Force that I thought he carried the whole weight of the armed services on his shoulders, he always found time to ask me how Hanady Investigations was doing and if I had any new cases.

Ellie was my partner in Hanady. She was the secretary, I was the treasurer, and we were both president. Ellie's family lived in the adjoining townhouse and our two families shared a porch. Her bedroom and mine were on either side of the same wall. We soon devised a complicated system of coded knocks. Three slow, three fast meant "Meet me on the roof at ten PM. Exciting news!"

We would both climb out our bedroom windows and meet in the middle of the overhanging porch roof. Wrapped in blankets, we would whisper about the amazing, adventure-filled lives we knew would be ours. We recorded every vivid detail in diaries we kept hidden under the eaves, wrapped in dry-cleaning bags.

Ellie was going to be a world-famous writer, traveling to exotic lands to discover unknown cultures. She would study them and write about the children living there. I was going to be a master detective, discovering secret underground tunnels and hidden passageways, helping kids find lost fortunes and locate missing parents. We thought our career choices were a perfect match for two ambitious ten-year-olds eager to explore the world.

We hatched our first case late one night on the rooftop. I called it *The Case of the Witch in Townhouse Two*. It would be embellished and refined over time, but the basic story line was that we had a witch living in one of the town-house apartments across the street from our own. We hoped to catch her casting spells on children, but we had never seen her up close. Kids who had lived in her six-unit apartment building had vanished. Grown-ups said that they had moved away, but we thought not. We tracked her movements from the military-issue two-man tent my dad set up in the yard for us, spying on her with military-issue binoculars.

We soon developed a plan to catch her. We decided to take advantage of Halloween to get inside her house and volunteered to take my four-year-old sister, Jan, trick-or-treating.

"Why, Valerie. How sweet of you," my mother said, surprised. I was not given to generosity when it came to younger siblings. Jan scowled at me. She might be young, but Jan was no fool.

"I don't *want* to go with her," she said, squirming as my mother adjusted her pumpkin costume and pulled on her green stocking cap. "She's mean."

This was a fair assessment. Vickie was the responsible older sister, even though she was only eleven months my senior. However, my standard line with Jan and Henry was "If you bump into me or talk to me or come near me, I'll kill you. So just stay away."

But now I needed Jan. I grabbed one of her hands and Ellie took the other. "Come on. We have to get going."

The night was cool and windy, blowing tatters of clouds across the full moon. When the moon's face was uncovered, you could just about pick out individual trees on the Chugach foothills. When the moon disappeared, the dark closed in and it seemed spooky—a perfect Halloween night.

We passed small knots of kids dressed as ghosts and witches or, more elaborately, as Batman, Cinderella and various Disney characters. We had been out for about an hour and had done quite well in the candy department. The big pillowcase bulged with candy—more than enough for the three of us.

Then Ellie and I eyed each other, knowing it was time to level with Jan. "We can count out all our candy and eat some," I said, "but first you have to help us with our investigation." Ellie took two extra-long jump ropes out of a paper bag and began to tie them together.

"No-o-o," Jan wailed. "Don't make me."

Jan knew the score. How the candy got split would depend on how helpful she was. I explained that we needed bait to entice the neighborhood witch to open her door. That bait would be Jan.

Ellie reached behind Jan to tie the jump rope around her waist. Jan kicked her a good one.

"Ow." Ellie rubbed her shin.

I reached slowly, slowly into the pillowcase. I extracted the biggest candy bar in the sack. I held it up in the moonlight, so that Jan could see it was the prize of prizes, the Holy Grail of candy bars, a Big Hunk bar. Slowly I peeled away the paper, strip by strip, banana-style.

"No-o-o—"

"Are you going to do it?" I moved the candy bar slowly toward my mouth. "Last chance." We had to get moving. I had bragged to kids at school that we would crack this case tonight, and the base curfew for kids was fast approaching. We needed documentation—at least a photograph of the witch, maybe huddled over her cauldron cooking up small animals and missing children.

Jan caved. We tethered her with the jump ropes so we could reel her in if the witch nabbed her. Our instructions to her were clear: "Smile, say trick or treat, then step inside and push the button on the top of the camera. Don't get into the oven or any big pot. Don't eat anything she gives you."

Ellie and I hid in the bushes, close enough to hear the soft knock, and Jan's "Trick or treat." Then, in one second, Jan was gone, and we heard sounds that could have been evil laughter from inside.

We yelled, "Take the picture!" and pulled on the rope with all our strength. We saw a flash of light and heard a *thunk* as Jan fell backward. We hauled her over the threshold. Ellie scooped her up and we ran.

We paused on the back porch to deal with the now-sniffling Jan before we went inside. Ellie tried to hug and comfort her. Ellie had no younger siblings, so she didn't know any better.

I knelt down and spoke face-to-face with Jan. I told her in graphic detail what would happen to her candy if she didn't fall in line. Ellie opened her back door and slipped inside and I pulled Jan into our apartment.

Mom picked Jan up and sat her on the kitchen counter. She was muddy, and her face was streaked with tears and snot.

"Sweetie, what's wrong?" Mom said. "What happened?" I poked my head out from behind Mom and stared at Jan.

"A witch gave me a poison apple."

"Oh, I bet there were a lot of witches out tonight," Mom said, brushing Jan's hair back. "Let's get you cleaned up. Say thank you to your big sister for taking you trick-or-treating."

Jan gave me a look of pure hatred. "Thank you," she said in a lisping voice that was far too deep for such a small child.

In a week we got the developed film back. We had a photograph of a pair of legs.

Disappointingly, our subject turned out to be a sort of surrogate grandma to the neighborhood. Not a witch at all.

Ellie and I retreated to the roof to work up another case, *The Mystery of the Haunted Ski Chalet*. We would investigate the case for months, but without Jan. She had discovered that screaming "No, Valerie, no! Don't hit me again!" got me in trouble and put her under Mom's protection—a sanctuary where she was, for a time, untouchable.

The setting for *The Mystery of the Haunted Ski Chalet* was a hut where Air Force skiers drank cocoa in winter, located on the base's ski run about five miles from our house. Empty and locked in summer, it would be a regular ghost-magnet, we thought. We were strictly forbidden to trespass on that particular site.

Obviously, calling something off-limits just made it desirable. Once, having been told to leave moose alone, we went on moose-hunting expeditions to photograph the ill-tempered and dangerous animals. We often explored the forbidden junkyard and snuck off-base to buy candy. But the chalet was our favorite, and I hiked there at least once a week to do surveillance with my siblings, Ellie and my cousin Carol. We made notes and drew up charts. I took pictures with my prized Kodak. Conveniently, there was a handy shortcut to the chalet from our house: the airfield landing strip. We usually cut across the tarmac, but once, to avoid technicians working on several planes, we tried the far end of the airfield, the cleared space beyond the pavement where the planes taxied if they couldn't stop in time. We decided to go one by one, so as not to draw attention.

The others hid in the bushes while I made the first crossing. I stepped onto what appeared to be solid ground to find it had the consistency of chocolate pudding. The quicksand mud pulled me down so fast that I sank to my knees before I could react. I yelled for help, and my sister and cousin just managed to pull me out, but the mud ate one shoe. Vickie stayed behind to try to find it as we headed for home.

I knew I would get in trouble for crossing the airstrip, so I pulled a diversionary tactic. I told Mom that I'd gotten stuck in quicksand and that Vickie wouldn't help me. Mean, mean Vickie had made me walk home with one shoe. When Vickie got home, she caught it for not taking care of me, her little sister—all of eleven months younger.

Considering some of the stuff we pulled on each other, it's amazing that we grew up to be the good friends that we are. We must have given Mom quite a workout.

When it came to Dad, though, everyone toed the line. My father was military, so what he said was law. It was never 6:00 PM at our house, it was eighteen hundred hours. From oldest to youngest, we answered the phone: "Sergeant Vanderwyk's residence."

Dad believed in hard work. He was a Master Sergeant, the highest rank an enlisted man could attain. His personal motto was "Don't call me Sir—I work for a living."

My brother and sisters and I worked in the garden, and we mowed the lawn. I figured out how to get around some of the work my sibs got stuck with. I developed "allergies," and even though I think Dad was on to me, he was charmed enough to let it slide.

We were similar, Dad and I, in some ways, and we were close. We were both adventuresome, creative and curious, but he was an engineer, and I couldn't even start the lawn mower. He taught Vickie to change tires and other "independent woman" stuff. He considered me a lost cause and gave me a buck to call him if I blew a tire.

When I was little, I thought he was the savior of the world. He was so busy that I thought it must be Dad who held the whole military together. That was why he had to be gone all the time, I just knew it. He couldn't tell us where he was going or how long he would be away. Sometimes he was even gone for Thanksgiving or Christmas.

He wasn't home on the afternoon of Good Friday, March 27, 1964, when Anchorage was rocked by a 9.2 earthquake—the strongest quake in US history. We were lucky. Our belongings were thrown all over the place, but our duplex wasn't seriously damaged. Somehow my dad got home from wherever he was. He literally walked in the front door, saw for himself that we were all right—even though everything in the house was all over the place and broken—gave us a quick hug, and left. We found out later that he had stopped by a neighbor's house and asked him to take us with him if there was a tsunami. Dad did this because he had to work. He was in charge of communications, and they had to get communications up and running.

We'd lived in Alaska several years, so we were used to little quakes, but this giant 9.2 quake was something else. In Anchorage there were building tops that were now even with the street. I remember being very impressed by a story that circulated about a brother and sister who had fallen into a crevasse that opened under them and then closed and swallowed them up. I had hoped that maybe our school would have to stay closed for a while, but no such luck.

By the time I was a teen and we were living in the Philippines, my dad was being sent not only into Vietnam to set up communications, but also into Cambodia and Laos—countries the United States wasn't even supposed to be in.

At the time, I was far too busy having fun to notice. I was a teenage girl sharing a military base with thousands of young men. Vickie and I were the queens of the universe. I had also turned into a smart-mouthed know-it-all. For a period of about three or four years, no one liked me. Fortunately I knew everything, so it didn't matter.

Dad told me I would make a good attorney because I liked to argue so much, but he wouldn't be drawn into the arguments. He'd just say, "Well, if that's the way you're going to be, take your plate upstairs and finish your dinner there."

When Boise became our permanent home after Dad retired in 1969, I was more than ready to put down roots. I graduated from Boise's Capital High School in 1970 and enrolled at Boise State University that fall.

In the spring of sophomore year, I met Jay. I remember the day well. March in Boise can fall backward into winter, but this day was so balmy that I was happy to soak up a little sun in Julia Davis Park next to the college. I leaned my bike against the bench to read another chapter in *Sisterhood Is Powerful*, a book about Women's Liberation that was provoking heated discussion, in class and out.

A shadow fell across the page. I looked up to see this really cute guy standing next to his bike. He'd been riding by, and when he saw me, he jumped off to take a closer look. I decided he might be worth a closer look too. He had beautiful long, straight hair, a trim beard and mustache, and he wore stylish granny glasses.

"My name's Jay," he said. "What's yours?"

"Valerie."

"What's your sign, Valerie? I think we could be compatible. Maybe it's fate that we met."

Oh no, I thought. *Not that corny line.* I was afraid he was about to add, "We must have known each other in a former life." But if he was, he fortunately thought better of it.

"Look," he said, "I think you're really beautiful. I just wanted to know if you still believe in dating, even though you're reading that book."

"Yes," I said, "but I don't date creeps."

That didn't scare him away. As we talked more, I found myself warming to his genuineness. It wasn't long before we rode off on our bikes together, a ride that soon led to a first date.

Maybe there really was an element of fate in our meeting. Jay later told me he had been humming the Monkees' song *Valleri* as he rode through the park just before we met. He had been unable to get the tune out of his head.

The more I got to know Jay, the more I liked him. For one thing, I really respected him for overcoming a tough childhood. His mom was out of the picture and Dad was a drunk. Jay was raised by an aunt and uncle in Sacramento. Periodically, Dad would turn up, claiming to be sober and ready to be a parent. Jay would go with his dad, and Dad would get drunk. When things got bad enough, he'd send Jay back to Sacramento.

One memorable Christmas Eve in a Nevada town, Dad took Jay to midnight Mass. Dad staggered up the aisle and refused to leave. A brawl ensued. Dad went to jail and eleven-year-old Jay slept the rest of that night on a cot outside Dad's cell. Not long after that, Jay was sent to Boise to live with his mother—a stranger to Jay.

By his own admission, Jay wasn't a great student. He and his mom battled through his teen years. When Jay graduated from high school, in 1969, he moved out and lived on his own. He enrolled in college that fall and by 1971 had earned a nursing degree.

Jay and I dated through the summer of 1972. It was a wonderful, magical summer. One hundred thousand people gathered in Washington, DC, to protest the Vietnam War, but we were not among them. Mark Spitz won seven gold medals at the summer Olympics, but Munich seemed very far from Idaho. We sang, "Bye-bye, Miss American Pie," as Don McClean's smash hit climbed the charts, but the theme of our own summer was not good-bye at all. It was hello. Hello to love, to the unique and private world we were creating together.

We hiked and biked. We went to football and basketball games. There was enough money for grilled cheese and french fries, with enough left over to see a movie. We took in *The Godfather*.

It wasn't long before we were pretty much inseparable. It seemed time for my parents to meet Jay. They invited us both for dinner one Friday night.

Jay dressed up for the occasion—in the manner of the day. Besides his signature granny glasses, he had on a leather vest with a lot of nice, long fringes, each fringe knotted with a bead. He had on his "dress" bell-bottoms, personalized with patches. He wore a selection of necklaces, several with peace signs.

My dad opened the door. My father, who retained much of the crispness of the career military man, found himself face-to-face with his daughter's beau, the bearded hippie.

I can only imagine the degree of self-discipline it must have taken—the stoicism fostered through decades of military service—for Dad to extend his hand and welcome Jay that first night. After he left, my folks were unusually terse. Dad told me it was probably a good thing to date different kinds of people so that I would know what to look for in a serious relationship when the time came.

But I was no longer interested in dating around. Dad and Mom soon saw a lot of Jay. We hung out at their house with my siblings and their kids, swimming in the pool and playing volleyball.

Long before the wedding day, my parents had come to appreciate Jay's good qualities. Underneath all that hair, he was smart, he was honest and he could be funny as heck. Time would reveal other qualities, too, like the loyalty that made him good for the long haul that is marriage.

Jay and I discovered our differences, of course. He was a local kid and I'd lived all over. Occasionally the disparity in our backgrounds showed. For instance, Jay sometimes assumed that local expressions were universal —that the whole world called a glove compartment a "jockey box," the way Idahoans did, and knew that a "borrow pit" was the ditch at the side of a road, from which the dirt to build the road was "borrowed." But those differences were minor compared to the core values we did share.

I'd never been someone who was preoccupied with getting married.

I wasn't even sure that marriage was for me. That changed when I fell deeply in love with Jay. We were married on May 25, 1973, fourteen months after we met. We held the ceremony at Christ Chapel, on the BSU campus. My uncle, a Presbyterian minister who was driving a taxi in San Francisco as a break from the ministry, officiated. Afterward, whenever I told the story, I would say that we'd been married by my uncle, the taxi driver.

We were newlyweds and we were college seniors living in an old trailer. We were poor, but we were so happy, we didn't know it. We got scholarships and grants, and Jay worked part-time selling medical equipment while I worked part-time at Macy's.

We both graduated in May 1974—I had a BA degree in social science and Jay got a BS in business. After we graduated, Jay took a job in Payette, a town about seventy miles northwest of Boise, and I became a caseworker there for Idaho's Child Protective Services. We both went to school at night, working toward our masters degrees.

That left plenty of time for us to get to know each other, and we had a little more money. We were a conservative-spending couple, but after we made the car payment and wrote a check for Jay's small student loan, we still had enough to take some great trips—several with my parents, who now began to seem more like adult friends.

Those first five years of marriage were a sweet time: one of the happiest of my life. I wasn't in a big rush to start a family. It wasn't until I turned twenty-five and had finally completed my MBA that it seemed like the time was right to have kids. To tell the truth, I hadn't gone into the marriage one hundred percent sure that I wanted children. I didn't think that I had a maternal nature. I didn't go all gushy over babies the way other women seemed to and I wasn't especially drawn to children.

I did have a thing for animals, though. I was nurturing as all get out when it came to Charcoal and Trouble, the two stray dogs we adopted. I just didn't connect the dots to realize that I was tapping into a latent vein of mother-instinct.

It was ironic in the light of my ambivalence, but the very first time we tried to make a baby, I became pregnant. I was immediately and completely awe-struck and thrilled. This wasn't just any baby, this was my baby. Our baby, Jay's and mine.

That night, I tried to act completely calm. I just kind of slipped it into the conversation: "How was your day? Oh, and by the way, I'm pregnant. I missed a period, so I went and got tested." But I couldn't keep up the casual front, I was too excited.

Jay grabbed me and waltzed me around. Then he stopped and stared at me like he was seeing me for the first time, or seeing me in a new light. I guess maybe he was.

"You're glowing," he said. "I thought that was just a figure of speech."

When we went to tell my folks, all my dad said, was "Ah . . . was this planned?"

Planned? We were five years and two masters degrees past the vows. We hadn't exactly leapt into this thing impulsively.

My family was actually quite thrilled—even my dad, once he got over the initial shock. It was fun to have another thing to cluck about with my sister Jan. We were on the phone 24/7, and she helped me to shop for maternity clothes. I was pretty convinced that I was having a girl, so we made the rounds of garage sales to find frilly outfits. I adored the teeny, tiny dresses and accessories—itty-bitty pink tights with ruffled bottoms, satin headbands embellished with rosebuds. I would arrange the outfits on my bed and imagine dressing my baby. I would call her Christine, which was a name I always chose when playing pretend as a child. If baby turned out to be a boy, he'd be Christopher.

I was full of plans. I would quit my job and stay home and raise our child. How hard could it be to raise a kid? Sure, I was a little short on firsthand experience, but I'd read about parenting and I'd talked to the experts. If, down the road, I encountered a problem I couldn't figure out on my own—well, I had a master's degree, didn't I? I knew how to do research. No *problemo*.

I was nauseated through the first trimester. I could just about choke down saltines and ginger ale. Then, at the start of my fourth month, Jay and I were hanging out and watching TV late one Friday night. Suddenly, I had a vision. I was in the clutches of a desire so strong as to be irresistible. I seized poor Jay by the lapels, pulling his face within an inch of my own.

"Chips. Must . . . have . . . barbecue potato chips."

Every night after that, at 10:00 PM, I'd send Jay out for Lay's KC Masterpiece Barbecue Potato Chips. My other food fetish was Campbell's Bean with Bacon Soup. I salivated at the thought of scraps of pig flesh floating on a red tomato sea. That was dinner and the chips were dessert. Nothing before or since has tasted like those chips.

The seventh month was the high-water mark of the pregnancy. I was becomingly with child, not yet the Goodyear blimpette I would be in a few more weeks. The end was in sight, but not so close that labor seemed real.

Jay and I took a Lamaze class for six weeks, overlapping my sixth and seventh months, at the end of which I took my mother out to lunch. Between the main course and dessert, I instructed her in childbirth.

Childbirth was a natural process, I told her, for which my female body was uniquely designed. My womanly inner wisdom would guide me through childbirth. I would also be empowered by learning how to focus and how to control my breathing, and then it wouldn't be pain that I felt, just sensation.

My mother delicately cleared her throat and patted her mouth with her napkin. "That sounds wonderful, dear," she said with a sweetly enigmatic smile.

After I had the baby, I told her, "Mom, I was in horrible pain. It was awful."

"I know," she said, "But I didn't want to tell you that."

She never did let me forget about that.

Christine was about two when Jay began working in the hardware and lumber industry. It proved to be a good fit for him, and he advanced in management. Over the next decade, two boys—Jeff and Scott—rounded out our family.

As the hardware companies Jay worked for were bought out, merged, and changed corporate headquarters, we moved—from Portland, Oregon, to Denver in 1988, then on to Western Pennsylvania in 1994, followed by a move to the Chicago area three years later.

I hadn't wanted a transient childhood for my children. I had wanted them to grow up in one house, where I would mark their height on the pantry wall each year, penciling in the dates so that someday their own children could see the marks.

Instead, I anchored my family in traditions we carried with us, like eating Cinnabons first thing on Christmas morning. We munched those gooey, sticky, sweet buns until they were gone, and no one thought about calories. We licked the icing from our fingers. Then there were the scratch tickets and the foil-wrapped chocolate coins that were stocking stuffers, year after year, in Oregon, Colorado, Pennsylvania, Illinois.

In each new house I set up my craft area. I collected supplies to make things for friends and for the kids, sometimes starting months in advance of a birthday or event. One Christmas, I made a life-sized igloo from cardboard boxes. Another Christmas project was a cardboard and tinfoil robot with drawers so the kids could store their toys.

We played cutthroat family games of Pictionary and Racko. We played killer practical jokes. Anyone who got me could expect retribution—not swift, but sure. Jay learned this early on when we were still young marrieds in Portland. Christine was maybe three or four. We were waiting for the tax return and we really needed it.

Jay was the one to pick up the mail. Every day, I met him at the front door and asked, "Did it come yet?" After a week of this, he came home one day looking truly gloomy. I asked him, "Did it come yet?"

"No," he said. "We got audited."

"Oh no. We counted on that money. What'll we do?" We had been holding on, just waiting for that check. What a disaster.

Jay pulled the government check from behind his back. "Gotcha."

I was so mad. I didn't care for that joke at all.

I waited six months, until Jay went out of town on a big business trip. He was working out of the house at that time, so he got a lot of mail at home. I went to work. I wrapped boxes, addressed manila envelopes and piled the phony correspondence in a mail mountain on his desk. Whenever he called, I said, "Boy, you are sure getting a lot of mail."

He caught a late flight home and he was just dragging by the time he got in.

"I've never known you to get so much mail," I said as he walked into the room. He just stared at the massive mound. It was taller than he was.

Finally, he said, "Well. I guess I better get started. So much for sleep."

"Oh, and by the way," I said, "we're being audited."

Jay groaned and fell backward onto the bed.

"Gotcha."

There were good jokes and bad jokes, good times and hard. Christmas followed Christmas. Summer brought picnics and pool parties. Fall always meant the start of school. Jeff advanced from play groups to soccer, basketball and football. Christine traded Girl Scouts for the dance squad. Scott went off to elementary school.

My kids learned to adapt to the moves, as I had. I tried to help them by always making new friends welcome. I gave them movie money or we rented video games. I gave them doughnuts to take to school—anything to help them seem cool. They found friends and good times, but it wasn't always easy.

I developed my own protocol for moving to a new place.

When I moved someplace, I didn't compare it to the place we had left, because it's insulting to the new town. If I wanted to fit in, I had to make myself love it. Since we were only going to be living there for a few years, I gave myself about four months to accomplish that. I looked for the good points to moving a lot. There are some. For instance, if you move every two to three years, then you don't have to clean under the refrigerator or the piano until the movers come to take them.

The one time I didn't follow my own protocol was when we moved to Butler, Pennsylvania, in 1994. Jay's company headquarters was located in that tiny town north of Pittsburgh and it was the one place I'd never wanted to go. Jay had sworn we'd never have to move there. Then the company assigned Jay to a job in Butler and so off we went. It just killed me to leave Denver.

We were moving to a tiny town. Butler had a steel mill, a car plant and the nation's second-most polluted waterway. Butler County had one claim to fame: The place had been the setting for *Night of the Living Dead*.

Great. Welcome to Butler, home of the living dead.

I was not thrilled. I was not going to be a good sport.

We scouted houses for several months and finally bought a place. It was a much bigger house than we could have afforded in Denver. Jay moved into the new place in advance of me and the kids, as usual. He used the time before we arrived to explore the town. He sampled the local eateries. He looked for a church.

In the course of the many moves, Jay and I had joined quite a range of Protestant and nondenominational churches. We were less interested in theology and ritual than in finding a spiritual home—that one church that felt right. When we found it, it didn't matter whether the church had a rock band or what color the carpeting was. When we found it, our family would truly be home. This was an important decision and so, in a new town, Jay and I would take our time and look around.

Not this time.

The kids and I arrived by plane early on a Sunday morning. Jay picked us up at the airport. We pulled up to our new house just as the moving van rolled up. We arrived in time to help unload the van. All of us carried in box after box, sorting them by label—bedroom, living room, kitchen cabinet, bathroom closet.

I really had moving down to a science. I gave the movers a diagram of each room so they knew where each box should go, and not just what room but what corner of the room.

After an hour of unloading, I dropped the last box of books and fell onto it. Taking their cue from me, the boys perched on boxes, but Christine sprinted to forage in Jay's bachelor fridge for a Coke. She held it up triumphantly.

"Last one."

"Split it," Jeff said.

I fanned myself with a newspaper. "Give it up for Mom."

"Here." Christine held the cold bottle to my warm forehead for a moment and then danced just out of reach.

"Rotten kid."

Jay bounded into the room, full of enthusiasm. Jay, who hadn't risen at 0-dark-hundred to catch a plane. He looked at his watch. "Hey, gang, it's only ten. We have time to clean up and make church. Let's check it out. What do you think?"

I thought about the four thousand boxes to be unpacked.

"Let's go." I sighed. "Afterward, we can see if this one-horse town has a Pizza Hut."

"All *right.*" Jeff and Scott were already moving toward the door. My kids were not above being bribed by pepperoni and extra cheese. As a matter of fact, neither was I.

The church turned out to be a stately brick edifice. The bright morning might have made the interior seem more cavernous and dark than it actually was, but it definitely wasn't cozy. As my eyes adjusted, I noted a serious pipe organ and ladies in hats.

So backward, I thought. In Denver no one wore a hat to church. In Denver you would be welcome in blue jeans.

The service had started, so we looked for an empty row. Every head swiveled to check us out. We were not a quiet group as we clonked and thunked our way down the wooden pew. I might be wrong, but I think the pastor actually paused a beat to wait for us.

We had no sooner settled in than Jay, without prior notice or discussion, stood up and announced that we wanted to join the church as a family. If Jay had glanced down at his family just at that moment, the row of horrified faces might have given him pause.

As I trailed up the aisle to officially join the church, sullen teens in tow, it occurred to me that it might be pleasant to smack him. I'd had to move to Butler and now I had no say about choosing a church. But, with the spotlight squarely on our family, I had to suck it up and hope my expression conveyed warm acceptance.

Jay grinned proudly as we filed back into our row and sat down. He fixed his gaze on the pastor, oblivious to the blast of death-ray dirty looks from the rest of us.

The sermon featured a moderate amount of fire and brimstone. At one point, the pastor asked us to close our eyes and imagine hell. I wrote on the back of my church bulletin, "We are in hell right now and you know whose fault that is," and passed the note to Christine, who nodded.

Christine was taking the move hard too. Because of the way the Denver schools were organized, she'd been at the same school for four years since seventh grade. The timing of the move was especially bad because she had tried out for the Denver dance team and had made the squad.

In Butler, my determined daughter went ahead and tried out for the dance team. Not knowing anyone, she still made the team. Over time, she made friends and so did I. All of us eventually became fond of that church, and Jay and I even stepped up to run the youth ministry.

Soon, the pastor and I were playing practical jokes on each other. He hit me with a water balloon. I waited two weeks, until his guard was down, and then gave Jeff and his youth group friends whipped cream pies. We followed the pastor out of church. I got him in the face first and then they nailed him. I only wish we'd documented the damage.

We did take advantage of being in the East. We took the kids to New York City and to Baltimore. We saw Niagara Falls and Cleveland. We probably saw more countryside than the Butler people who had always lived there.

Within a year, Butler was as much home as Portland and Denver had been.

By the time Jay's company merged to form a larger entity with headquarters in Chicago, I was reluctant to leave my church family and my comfortable home. Christine chose to stay and finish college in Pennsylvania.

What I didn't know, as I packed for Chicago, was that our two decades of wandering were nearly over. We had moved in an arc, from west to southwest, then east and north. Soon we would close the circle, turning west toward Boise and home.

When we did return to Boise, in July 1999, we came home in style. The hardware cooperative Jay had worked for as marketing manager laid him off with a year's salary and all moving expenses. No sooner had we made the move than he was offered a great job in Boise.

Scott would be a sixth grader, and Jeff would be a high school sophomore. We'd already enrolled them and I was proud that they would attend Christian schools for the first time. I thought we deserved parenting points for using money that could have paid for a ski vacation in Switzerland instead to further their education.

Our house was in a quiet cul-de-sac close to the schools. I was adept as ever at transforming a new house into our home. Touches like strategically placed throw rugs and willow baskets overflowing with dried flowers gave the place a rustic, country flavor.

Although our house was located in a development, Boise was a Western city that bumped up against the wilderness. It wasn't like the Chicago we had left behind, a city that seemed to stretch forever in every direction. If I went to the end of our block and turned right, I would pass tons of other subdivisions that could compete with ours for the title of suburbia's most suburban subdivision, but if I turned left, I soon ran out of road.

If I parked at the wooden barrier that marked the end of the pavement and walked a little farther, I soon lost sight of everything but the rolling hills that merge into Boise National Forest—more than two million acres of treed slopes that rise to the southern flank of the Sawtooth Range, where jagged peaks blend into another range and beyond that, into more mountains. Living close to wild country was another reason to be happy about the move, as far as I was concerned. I enjoyed the beautiful setting enormously and it was also a reminder of my childhood years in Alaska.

We spent much of that July and August at my sister Jan's pool. I worked on my tan, and my sons played in the water with their cousins or befriended whatever lucky stray dogs Jan happened to have on hand. I shopped with Mom and had lunch with my older sister, Vickie. I tackled a few low-key projects. I made a cardboard jungle for the Safari Vacation

Bible School sponsored by Capitol City Christian Church, which was the nondenominational North Boise church my extended family attended.

I soon felt comfortable at Capitol City. I loved the combination of the beautiful old building—with exquisite stained glass panels—and the contemporary service. It had upbeat music and was relevant to daily life. I liked the people.

When the boys went back to school in the fall, I held a few piddly, part-time jobs. I got involved in more activities at church.

I loved my life. I lived where I wanted to live; I had a happy marriage—notwithstanding the ups and downs of any long-term relationship—and the kids were in basically good shape. They were still too young, in any case, to have gotten into serious trouble. They were still young enough to think that I was the coolest mother in the world. Things were about as perfect as they were ever going to be.

And then I found the lump.

Chapter 2

The Cancer Advantage

I MIGHT HAVE BEEN PLANNING A CENTERPIECE FOR the Thanksgiving table, or I could have been thinking ahead to Christmas and the video game Scott wanted. The truth is, I can't remember exactly what I was thinking about, while I did my routine breast self-exam in the shower that morning. I was moving my fingertips in the widening concentric circles when I felt a lump in my right breast. It was about the size of a pea.

Over the years, I'd found other lumps and they'd all been harmless, but I decided I'd go in so I wouldn't worry about it. I knew they were going to say it was nothing. I knew that setting up an appointment with a new gynecologist would take a few days though, so I did call right away.

When I showed up for the appointment, the doctor seemed a nice enough woman and I liked her nurse. After examining me, the doctor said, "I don't think it's something we need to be worried about."

I should have felt relief, but instead, I was frustrated. My mammogram indicated that there was nothing to be concerned about, but now

I had a gut feeling that something was wrong. Something about this lump set off alarm bells.

"I know it's not something we need to worry about." I crossed my arms over my chest. "It's me who's worried. You'll go home and sleep tonight. *I'll* be the one who's worried."

The doctor took a needle biopsy in her office and sent it off to be evaluated.

"Let's just watch it," the doctor said as she pulled off her latex gloves.

"No." I said, "Let's not 'watch it.'" I insisted on an ultrasound, but the test was not definitive. The more they pressured me to back off, the more I pushed to find out the truth.

I'd learned the hard way that you had to be assertive with doctors.

I'd been through this before, when my children had faced life-threatening illnesses. I had been able to tell right away something was wrong with newborn Christine as soon as I held her. She couldn't keep anything down; nothing was going through her system. Doctors told us her intestines were incompletely formed. She couldn't eat. They whisked her away to the Neonatal Intensive Care Unit.

At the time, I was a brand-new mom. Every instinct, every nerve-ending, was sending the same message: Hang onto that baby. When I couldn't, it was horrible. Jay put an arm around me and I think a nurse had my other side. They led me to the NICU and there was Christine, a hostage in a glass box, pinned down in a tangle of tubes, wires and monitors. I had to tell myself over and over, "It's helping her, it's helping her," so I wouldn't freak out. She was so tiny and she looked so sick.

We met with the surgeon and he told us she needed surgery, a gastric bypass like you'd get to lose weight. This bypass would cut out the section of unformed intestine. Christine was less than a day old when she had this major surgery. She spent the next three weeks in the NICU.

At that time, the medical establishment believed that newborns couldn't feel pain because their nervous systems were not fully developed. Therefore, they prescribed no postoperative painkillers for Christine. She cried inconsolably. I knew something wasn't right.

I was still terribly naïve. It's very challenging when your firstborn faces illness. You're barely used to being a parent, and you are forced into a situation where your decisions could mean life or death.

Christine's doctor, who looked like he might be all of thirty, seemed determined to avoid conversation with the family members of his small patients. I spent a day on the lookout for him, but I only caught a few glimpses as he flashed by the end of a long corridor, and once I saw him whisk into an elevator.

All right, I thought, *two can play this game.* The next day, I lay in wait for him around the corner of the Neonatal Intensive Care Unit. When he sprinted by, I jumped out and literally ambushed him. Eventually, through sheer perseverance, I got him to tell me what was going on with my daughter.

Christine had to be fed every hour and she had to be held upright after every feeding, but she did recover. We brought her home from the hospital, and Christine's rocky start became little more than a family anecdote, a story I'd share about facing life's challenges.

But then Jeff was born. By the time he arrived in 1983, we were settled in Portland and Christine had grown into an independent child who already showed signs of the determined adult she would become. Little brother Jeff was a beautiful baby, lively and bright. He walked early and acquired language easily. At a year and a half, he spoke in sentences.

I had no reason to think that his eighteen-month "well baby" checkup in August 1984 would be anything more than a quick chat with a friendly pediatrician, a rite of passage marking the change from baby to toddler.

I remember that the doctor let Jeff play with the stethoscope while he palpated his little tummy. Jeff, that smart little monkey, already knew to put the end up to the doctor's chest. The doc was playing along by taking big breaths. Suddenly, I was aware that the doctor had stopped breathing. Or so it seemed. His hands, which had been moving over Jeff's torso had honed in on one spot.

"I'd like to take an X-ray to check Jeff's abdomen," he said. "In all likelihood, it's nothing. I just want to make sure."

I wasn't too worried. Obviously, Jeff didn't have Christine's problem. Jeff was, it seemed to me, the epitome of a healthy kid.

"I'll call down to the lab. You can go right on down." He smiled, reassuringly. "They'll take a look and then we'll know it's nothing."

We waited in the lab waiting room while they developed and looked at the film. I was called into a side room where a big light box spanned the wall. The nurse closed the door behind me. They hung Jeff's film up, and the radiologist and my pediatrician studied it intently. The neon light made both men look pale.

The pediatrician turned to me and started without preamble. "I was hoping we wouldn't find this." He shook his head. "Jeff has a neuroblastoma. Stage III. You can see, here, where it is." He pointed at the film.

I could see for myself that it was the size of a grapefruit and had little fingers all the way into his legs, entwined with all the nerves, veins and arteries.

Jeff would be dead within three months, the doctor said.

I fell to my knees with the pain of it. Even now, I can't imagine worse pain. I thought about suicide. I would drive off the bridge with Jeff in the car so I could die with him and he wouldn't have to suffer. But then I'd have to have Christine in the car, because I couldn't leave her without a mother. But what about Jay? That wouldn't be fair to him. He'd have to be in the car too. I'd have to sedate them all so they'd be willing, and I'd drive off the bridge. Then I realized that was all going to be too much work.

Joking about murder and suicide might seem strange, but black humor helped me cope. I had to get a grip. Jay and I linked arms to face whatever would come. Our Christian faith had always been a strong part of our lives and never more than now. We searched out a church prayer group and prayed along with them.

Jeff had surgery at Dornbecker Children's Hospital in Portland. We moved back to Boise for family support, and Jeff had radiation and chemotherapy at Mountain States Tumor Institute there. Tests showed that the tumor was unchanged. We returned to Portland for the second surgery, which was to be only exploratory, so the doctors could learn about the disease.

The day before the surgery, we went to nearby Beaverton to have Bettie Mitchell pray over Jeff. Bettie is known as a woman of strong faith. The walls of her office were covered with photographs of people from all over the world who had been helped by her Good Samaritan Ministries.

By then, Jeff had had enough of doctors and all other strangers. He ran around her office and played with things.

"I'm not going to pray until Jeff's ready," Bettie said. "I'm waiting for him to trust, because he and I have to be in agreement for healing to occur."

We sat there for what seemed like forever. I was consumed by fear. I couldn't get the CAT scan of the tumor out of my mind. Bettie let Jeff do what he wanted, and every ten or fifteen minutes she asked him if he was ready yet.

At the end of two hours, Jeff climbed onto her lap. She held his hands together with hers and said a simple prayer that Jeff could understand: "Dear Father, this is Jeff. Jeff is sick and he needs You to help him. Please help him."

The next day Jeff had surgery. They opened him up and in just two hours, the surgeon came zipping into the waiting room. "We got it all," he said, and kept on going, right out the door. No other doctor or nurse approached us. What did that mean: "We got it all"? We were in a kind of shock, because the reality we knew—Jeff had inoperable, Stage III cancer—had been turned on its head with no explanation. We couldn't really take it in and no one bothered to try to help us understand.

The surgeon never did speak with us. Neither did anyone else—not officially, anyway. That evening, when I was alone by Jeff's bedside, the resident who had assisted with the surgery stuck his head in the door. He cleared his throat a few times. I thought it was odd, but everything had been odd that day.

Finally he said, "I think I should tell you, because someone should, that we removed no cancer. There wasn't any there. All that was there was scar tissue."

Now I was really confused.

I said, "But you saw the CAT scan from the day before. It was all over."

"Well, I don't know what to tell you," he said. "Everyone's pretty baffled. Your son was sick and now he's better. No one has a clue why. I'm sorry."

He seemed embarrassed. It was almost as if the disappearance of Jeff's tumor was kind of an awkward thing for them, because they couldn't explain it. They made us feel like it was tacky of us to still be underfoot, where they could trip over us and be reminded of how much they didn't know.

Jeff was released from the hospital within a couple of days. We would never know if he had experienced some kind of spontaneous remission or been cured by the power of prayer. Had his superiors known, that kind resident would probably have been barred from the field for having a conscience and helping us out.

Of course it was wonderful to bring our son home. Relief and gratitude dominated those first days. Then—amazingly soon, really—gratitude was subsumed by daily life, and Jeff's illness and recovery were pushed to the back of my conscious mind. His illness and recovery helped shape his character. Jeff grew into a young person with an unusual degree of compassion for people who were hurting, especially children.

But one thing did not fade, and that was the distrust I had developed for the medical profession. I was much less inclined to accept things a doctor said on faith. This hard-won skepticism was my ally in the fight for my own life.

I wanted my breast lump to be evaluated further. At my insistence, my gynecologist sent me to a surgeon. He said the mass didn't feel like cancer, but he did a lumpectomy, a limited surgery to remove the lump. I woke from the outpatient procedure still a little groggy, but aware enough to notice that no one was telling me it was all fine. There wasn't any of that reassurance. Shortly, the surgeon came in, sat down beside me and took my hand. Then I knew. The news was bad. I had cancer.

The surgery had not removed it all, he told me. There was still cancer outside the margin of the lumpectomy. I was scared, of course. I had had so many lumps, so many double and triple mammograms to check, and they had all turned out fine. This time, it was for real.

But along with the shock was something like recognition. There has been a lot of breast cancer in my family. Both grandmothers, the aunts on both sides of the family, and several of my cousins had had it. My sister Jan had been through it. Only my mother and Vickie had been spared.

Around that same time, I had casually picked up a brochure that described a new genetic test. The test identified BRCA1, a gene mutation that predisposes women to breast cancer. I tossed the brochure. I didn't want to think about the possibility that I might fall into that high-risk category.

I found it heartening that my aunts, cousins and my sister were survivors. The fact that they were all still on the planet made me feel a little better. I didn't think that I had received a death sentence. I thought, *"Dang, I have to lose my hair. I have to lose a breast. I have to be sick for months."*

It was harder on Jay. He was completely brokenhearted. He couldn't handle it at all. He just fell apart. He couldn't even go in and talk to the doctor about the test results. As the weeks went by, I found myself comforting him.

My diagnosis affected every family member; each of my children confronted my illness in a characteristic way.

Scott ran from trouble. He asked me how I was and then he ran out the door. He didn't want to be left out, but he didn't want to be too far in.

Sixteen-year-old Jeff was my mainstay. He was the one who sat and prayed with me when Jay was out of town. He was the one who took care of me when I got chills or a cold. He was there when I was depressed or anxious—because of course I was. I kept having little anxiety attacks.

I didn't know that was why I was tired and wired at the same time. I'd never had anxiety before.

Christine, the golden girl, the perfect child, was upset that she couldn't be home to help. She was off at college and missed the worst of it by not being home on a day-to-day basis. I told her I felt all right, that she didn't have to see how awful I looked—no hair and all.

I decided to have a mastectomy rather than an extensive lumpectomy. I wanted to have the whole mess over and done with. I scheduled the mastectomy for right after Christmas. The operation went well, but they did find cancer in four lymph nodes.

I had done a lot of research into alternative therapies, like drinking green tea and wheatgrass. While those alternative medicines might be helpful for some people, they were not going to cure me of cancer, I decided. I began chemotherapy.

Chemotherapy had made Jan so sick that no one would believe that I didn't feel awful. They were convinced that I was just being unnecessarily brave when I said I felt fine, but I wasn't. I like to whine as much as anybody and I want sympathy as much as the next one. The fact is, most of the time I felt physically all right, through the six weeks of radiation and then the five months of chemotherapy. But the chemo—and all the steroids they gave me so I wouldn't have a bad reaction to the chemo—made me gain weight. I gained twenty-five pounds. When I complained about that to the doctors, they scolded me. "We're not a fat farm or a weight loss program," they said. "We're here to save your life."

Jan stepped into the role of chief organizer and helper. She took charge, she drove me everywhere. I relied on her completely. Jan was my official watchdog with the doctors and nurses. On the way to appointments, I told her, "Be nice," because I knew her. She had worked repossessing cars and other items for a local bank.

She was tough. Without actually coming out and saying so, she could convey the impression that if she so much as suspected that the care I was getting was one tick off optimal, the offender could expect to find himself dangling from the nearest open window.

It's a good thing she wasn't around for my last conversation with my gynecologist. She called the day I got home from the hospital after the mastectomy.

She said, "Hi, how are you doing?"

And I said—assuming that she was asking about the mastectomy, because the reports had been sent on to her—"Well, you know, I feel pretty good."

She said, "Here's something that's going to cheer you up even more. The needle biopsy came back clear."

I was silent for what seemed like two minutes. I realized that she had missed the cancer with the needle. She didn't know I'd had surgery, which had to mean she hadn't even read the report on me that the hospital had sent to her. If I hadn't insisted on further evaluation, I would have gone untreated. Finally she said, "That's a good thing."

I was angry enough to mess with her. I said, "No, it's not. Either you're wrong and I had to have a mastectomy you didn't tell me I needed, or you're right and I just lost my breast for no reason. Which one is true?" I never went back to that doctor.

For the next six months, I was consumed by the world of cancer. When you're being treated, it's like you're not *you* anymore. You're the Cancer Patient. Nothing else matters. You're cocooned in that world of cancer. The chemo wing is the center of your universe; everything you need is there. There's the Coke machine and ice. You can watch TV in your own little treatment room. You can sleep, you can read. You can yell to the nurses from your room, because it's open on one end.

They're the whole world, those nurses.

My family were with me a lot in the hospital, especially Jan. But I had just moved to the community when I got sick, so I had no support system of friends. The vacuum was filled by the nurses, who became my friends. They took care of me. They brought me lunch and goodies from the cafeteria. I brought them little gifts from home. They talked to me and sometimes they gossiped with me. I heard about their boyfriends and their husbands. I knew their children's names and where they were in school.

I got especially close to Maggie, a nurse who was not only my own age but who shared my birthday. The first day I came for the infusion she was there, a sturdy gal topped with a bunch of curly, red-gold hair, her round face sprinkled with freckles like a kid. She had a sarcastic edge that I liked.

I was in the market for distraction that first morning. I perched nervously on the big armchair in my roomette while they prepped me for the PICC (peripherally inserted central catheter) line. The PICC is one way of delivering the chemotherapy to your innermost insides. It's a plastic tube that is threaded through one of the larger peripheral veins—in my case, a vein in my upper left arm—all the way to a large vein near the heart. I was working hard not to visualize this procedure.

"I'm Margaret Noonan. That's 'Maggie' to you," the red-headed nurse said, as she swabbed my arm with disinfectant. "'Mags' also works. In case you were wondering, my ancestors were Russian." She pronounced it "Rooshan."

"And to think I had you pegged as Irish," I said. "Shows you what I know."

"Oh, I'm more Irish than the Irish. I'm from Southie." She arranged the surgical drapes over my arm. She tapped the prominent vein in the crook of my undraped arm. "These are veins I love, because they make inserting IV and PICC lines so easy. You could have a whole career with veins like these, just going around and making nurses happy."

"I'm willing to consider another career," I said, while the aide stared at us, google-eyed. "I've done the mom thing and I've been a social worker."

"Right," said Maggie. "You have lots of time for a third career and a fourth one after that. I'm never wrong about these things."

She looked at me directly and smiled. I returned her smile with true warmth, because she was telling me I would live. She was encouraging me without being patronizing. Maggie was a bracing astringent in a world that could pour on the sweet stuff a little heavy for my taste.

For instance, there was the staff at one of my doctors' offices. This doctor kept a photographic record of each patient. During my appointment, just after they had learned I had cancer, they took the standard photo, but instead of filing it, they ran around showing it to all the people in the waiting room and even to staff in the orthodontist's office across the hall, saying, "What a *cute* picture, isn't that darling, doesn't she look just like a model? Isn't she just the prettiest patient *ever*?"

Finally they convinced even me. I brought home a copy of the picture and shoved it under the nose of various family members, who basically said, "Yes, it is a picture of you. And . . . ?"

Maggie was there the day my hair fell out.

It didn't all come out at once. It was a few weeks into the infusions, and I had already decided that when the part at my crown widened to an inch, I would shave my head and get a wig.

Maggie was with me when I realized that I had reached my own milestone. It was time for the rest of my hair to go.

I stared into a hand mirror at the swollen, soon-to-be-bald stranger I had become and started bawling. I felt like the world's biggest baby, but I didn't care. Wonderful Maggie pried the mirror gently from my shaking fist and pulled up a chair alongside my recliner.

"You know," she said, thoughtfully, "the wigs they make now are so convincing that even you can't tell it's not your hair. Or, you could do something wild. Pick a style you would never think to try."

"Oh, you can too tell the difference," I blubbered. "A wig looks like a *wig*."

She was able to calm me down and helped me figure out what kind of new hairstyles I might like to try out.

My hair would eventually grow back and I would lose the twenty-five pounds I had gained. Meanwhile, I acquired four wigs, including several that were gifts. One of them was a perky hairdo that made me look like a cheerleader.

I did always want to be a cheerleader.

The nurses did everything they could to make chemo treatment better. One day a guy gave everyone foot massages. The next week a man brought in a guitar, and he and his wife sang sea chanteys. When I wasn't sleeping off the Benadryl they gave me to prevent side effects, it wasn't so bad.

Of course, there were the really sick people. I tried not to think about them or what it would be like to be one of them. I prayed I'd never be in that position.

My chemo schedule was three weeks on and one week off. I knew the schedule, but I wasn't tracking time too well. I had "chemobrain," which is the temporary mental fog that descends on about one-third of the people who have chemotherapy. So I'm not sure of the sequence of events, but one day Maggie came to talk to me at the end of her shift.

"I know I'm on the schedule, but I won't be in tomorrow," she said and then she burst into tears.

Maggie had to attend a memorial service for a close friend, she said. Plus, her brother had been diagnosed with liver cancer.

I got up and wrapped her in a hug.

"I know too much," she said. "I wish I didn't know all the things that I do. But you don't get to unknow them. He wants me to tell him it's going to be all right." She burst into tears again. "I'm sorry, I'm sorry to lay this on you. It's so unprofessional."

"Don't you dare be sorry." It felt incredibly good to give something back. "Don't you dare."

On my last day of treatment, I checked in just like always, handing the receptionist my plastic ID card like the old hand I had become. I scanned the waiting room for newbies. There was one: a scared-looking woman clutching her coat across her chest.

"Hi, I'm Valerie," I said. "They are so nice here. They make it easy. You'll be fine." She nodded uncertainly.

In the infusion center, I made the rounds, greeting staff and patients. I had picked up an orange coffee cake at Albertson's for the nurses, which I cut up in the unit kitchen. I passed out magazines I'd brought from home. Another patient gave me an article on cancer and nutrition she had been telling me about. A nurse took me aside to say that over the weekend her boyfriend had apologized up one side and down the other, just like I'd said he would, and they'd gotten back together and what did I think?

In other words, I felt like I was at home. After five months, this place was a familiar world, but I was still glad to be almost done.

I slept through the last hour of my final infusion. As I came to, I heard someone say, "Ah, let her wake up, first."

I was groggy, but I opened my eyes. I looked up to see Maggie. She was holding a cowbell, and there were people behind her.

"We're here to ring you out," she said. She recited the poem I'd heard read for other patients: "Ring this bell, three times well, the toll to clearly say: My treatment's done. The course is run. And I am on my way."

Then the place erupted in cheers and applause, and people crowded even closer—doctors, nurses, technicians and every patient who wasn't tethered to an IV.

Maggie unhitched me from my very last infusion and ceremonially presented me with the cowbell.

"Need more cowbell," she said. "Ring the bell." I rang the heck out of the thing while an intern led an impromptu conga line, chanting, "Val is done with che-mo, Val is done with che-mo." There aren't many times in my life when I've been more excited.

Then it was over. I had thought I would be thrilled to be done with treatment, but now I felt lost. Now what? Cancer had ripped through my world like a tornado. When I emerged from the storm cellar, I found my life wiped clean of familiar landmarks.

In 2000, cancer was still sort of a secret, a sorry-it's-happening-to-you-but-you-should-go-die-over-in-the-corner-and-be-quiet situation because it was so uncomfortable for people.

Talking to people about it was uncomfortable for me, too, because the first thing someone would do when you told them you had breast cancer was to stare at your chest. Or, you could feel them trying not to stare at your breasts. You just knew they were dying to ask, "So. Did you or didn't you? Are they yours or what?"

I didn't have the inner resources to rebuild after cancer. I felt empty. I followed Jan around, trying to reclaim some part of myself. Her friends became my friends. Actually, I was sort of a second-class friend, one person removed.

Jan suggested maybe I could take up knitting.

I didn't think knitting was the answer, but I wasn't sure what was. I was having a tiny identity crisis. I'd spent the last twenty years raising children, and while I was in no way sorry for that, and while I loved them all to distraction, I had spent most of my time focused on other people's needs. Now, not only did I have to figure out who the post-cancer Valerie was, I had figure out what I wanted to do with my life.

I sat down with a yellow legal pad and made a list of all the things I could become. I told myself to just write, without second-guessing myself. I would exclude no fantasy. I put cheerleader at the head of the list, since my perky wig made me look the part. I would also make a good dancer, I decided. That was something I loved and actually did well, in an amateur, ballroom-dancing kind of way. Maybe I would just bump it up a notch and go pro.

I listed vocalist, even though my family members are the kind of singers who get kicked out of choirs. I would not let mere lack of talent stand in my way. I imagined myself at the opening of the Super Bowl.

The celebrity chosen to sing the national anthem would be drunk. She would lurch onstage, singing way off-key. The crowd would grow restless and there would be a spattering of boos. Somehow, I would find my way onstage. I'd put out my hand and take the mike. I'd launch into a flawless "Star Spangled Banner," clambering up and down that octave-and-a-half like a kid on a jungle gym. I wouldn't even need the mike. By the time the bombs were bursting in air, there'd be nary a dry eye. I'd bring it on home, a fantastic display of fireworks would shoot color into the sky behind me, and the crowd would go wild.

Another longtime fantasy was being crowned Miss America, but I thought I could make do with Mrs. America, if it came down to it. You still need to walk the runway with an armful of roses and wear a tiara. People would admire my poise, my savoir faire. For the talent portion of the contest, I would sing. In French. I added it to the list, along with "take French lessons."

But what about the visual arts? I thought. I was already a crafter. Grandma Moses didn't started painting until she was in her seventies, I reasoned. I would take classes and wow the instructors. They would say to the younger students, "Go look at Mrs. Agosta's drawings if you want to learn something." The word would spread that a late-blooming genius had come to light—in Boise, yet. I imagined my awed family saying to the myriad of interviewers, "We simply had no idea she was so talented. We could never see past her beauty."

When I had burned through every outrageous fantasy I could possibly concoct, I started to think about paid occupations that attracted me. I didn't have to have a job, so I decided to look for something fun that I could do part-time. I considered and discarded events planning, catering, running a B and B, and being a veterinary assistant.

Then I remembered Nancy Drew.

I had always loved to solve mysteries, to hunt down information and put together clues and find answers. I had always loved to see the truth come to light and the bad guys put away.

Suddenly, I knew what I was supposed to do. I was going to become a private investigator.

Chapter 3

Two Moms in a Minivan

BEFORE MY HAIR HAD GROWN IN, I WAS WELL ON my way to becoming one of Boise's first female private investigators.

Not long after I had my Nancy Drew epiphany, I called Jan.

"I am so stoked," I said. "You can't believe what I'm going to do."

"Wha-at?" I heard, in Jan's drawing out of the interrogative, a shade of caution.

"Look, this is going to be so cool. I'm going to be a private investigator, and I would love it if you wanted to be involved. It would be such a blast, Jan. We'll be the snoop sisters."

No jump ropes. This would be a fifty-fifty deal between grown-ups.

"It can work, Jan. We can afford to be selective about the cases we take, because we wouldn't have to pay the mortgage or feed our families with it. If we don't want to take a case, we'll turn it down."

"Well, I think it does sound like it could be interesting," Jan said. "I don't really know what's involved. We would probably need to be licensed. I mean, I assume that we would have to be. I'm not prepared to do a whole lot of work on it. Check it out and let me know."

"I'll do the legwork," I said. "I'll find out what we need to do."

I did a little research and learned that PI licensing requirements varied by state. Idaho was one of seven states that did not require a license. However, we would have to be licensed, because Ada County, where Boise is located, required it.

I also learned that there were only a very few kinds of investigation that demanded extensive, specialized training. If I were interested in corporate investigation or computer forensics, I would do well to get an accounting degree or study computer science. Since I didn't find either of those areas compelling, I would do what most investigators did and learn on the job.

Jan came to the spy business already trained, in a sense. At the bank she worked for, she had handled collections for a decade. Today, financial institutions farm out collections, but back then, not only did she track loans in arrears, Jan was a repo gal — the one to go out in the middle of the night and personally take back the cars.

As it turned out, it wasn't hard to get licensed as a private investigator. We had to meet just five requirements. We needed three people to swear we were relatively normal and trustworthy. Jan was forty-two and I was forty-eight, so we met the age requirement. It only cost twelve dollars for the application fee. That just left being fingerprinted and finding photographs for an ID.

I didn't realize they meant I should get passport-type photos taken. I cropped two nice pictures taken at Christmas. The guys behind the counter at the licensing bureau thought the photos of me in my Christmas sweater were a hoot, but they accepted them.

To get fingerprinted, I put on my best wig, got a fresh manicure, and headed to the county courthouse. There, I was directed to stand in line under a sign that read Sex Offenders Register Here.

It was noon, and the line was unbelievably long. I tried to ignore the stares from passersby. I knew they were trying to figure out what heinous thing I'd done. I concentrated on a particularly interesting scuff-mark on the tip of my left shoe.

I zoned out. I don't know whether one minute passed or twenty. At some point, I noticed that just north of my own shoes were ten red toe-nails showcased in sling-backs. My eyes traveled up the pressed, form-fitting jeans, and over the cashmere sweater to a perfectly made-up face. Not one hair was out of place, and there were carefully applied high-lights. She looked very nice, I thought.

She smiled. My impression was knocked sideways. Her teeth were rotted stumps. It was a sight that would become all too familiar, but at the time, I had no idea what a meth mouth was.

She, in turn, was looking me up and down.

At last she asked, "Why are you here?"

Head high, I proudly said, "I'm going to be a PI."

"Right," she said, and snickered like it was the lamest excuse in the world for being on this line. "Hey, Adam." A knot of guys lounging in a row of metal folding chairs turned our way. "*She's* here to become a PI." They laughed like I was a joke on two legs.

Great. I was a middle-aged soccer mom in a purple sweatshirt with bunnies and the slogan "Sow the seeds of friendship," yet these strangers found it easier to believe I was a sex offender than a PI.

More people in the line turned around to stare.

I whisked the wig from my head and heard a raised voice that could not be my own, yelling, "I have *cancer*. I've been through hell. I've lived through chemo. I've lived through radiation. If I can beat a life-threatening disease, I can be a private investigator."

Shocked silence.

"Move aside, because I'm going to the head of this line." I started to move toward the counter. "Right now or I'll throw up all over you."

The sex offenders fell back and I stepped deliberately through the wide-eyed multitude, holding my wig before me like a scepter.

I realized at that moment that cancer had changed me.

I had been a shy girl who found her best friend in a book. Then I grew into a young woman who cared very much what people thought of her and was always measuring herself against others. Everyone wants attention, but it's hard when you're shy, because you want that attention—but at the same time, you don't. When I walked into a room, I checked to see if I was the best-dressed, the prettiest, the brightest. And since there was always someone with more, I was down on myself a lot.

I hated public speaking so much that I got around making the mandatory oral presentation that was required for my master's degree by convincing my professor that I was too busy to do it. I was an A student, so he let it slide. After college, I wouldn't take a job if it meant I had to speak in public.

Now I discovered that cancer had changed all that. Facing cancer was so big it made ordinary fears seem small. I might be mutilated, burned, poisoned and bald, but I had survived.

In some ways, I was more alive after cancer. I discovered that being a survivor conferred a certain freedom. I had decided, at age forty-eight, to emulate my childhood heroine Nancy Drew and become a private investigator, and I no longer cared what anyone thought.

Jan got her license and we dubbed ourselves Two Moms in a Minivan. We agreed to keep Hanady Investigations as our official name. We did not establish ourselves as a legal partnership. We really didn't see the need for that structure, nor did we rent an office.

We soon realized that our investigative styles were different, and reflected our personalities.

I was like the goofy younger sister, even though I am six years older. Jan fit the profile of the responsible older sib. She played a prominent role in church—she was head of the children's ministry and she was head of the women's association at the private school that was part of the church. I was sort of her sidekick. Maintaining her dignity was important to Jan. She cared very much that we be perceived as professional and organized. She wanted to study and to plan everything in advance. She didn't want to proceed until we had a full-fledged business plan.

I played Lucy to her Ethel. I wanted to jump in. I wanted to have fun, make my mistakes, and learn by doing. I didn't see the need for an office or a ton of formal paperwork. In fact, a major reason that I found the PI gig attractive in the first place was that it didn't have to be bureaucratic. It left a lot of room to be creative.

I had more room in my life for creativity than Jan, not only because my children were older than hers, but also because I really had two businesses going. At the same time that I started Hanady, I bought into Boise-based Death by Murder, a theater company that put on murder mystery parties in corporate settings. It would be a year before I got really involved in that group, though. For the present, I focused on getting Hanady off the ground.

We began reading how-to books like *The Complete Idiot's Guide to Private Investigation* and *How to Be Your Own Private Investigator.*

We studied the real-life stories of people who were private investigators. For research, we used Google, because we hadn't yet found our way to the kind of databases the pros used.

I didn't tell my extended family a whole lot about the business to start with. They were already convinced the chemo was making me a little nuts. While it was kind of fun to have them slightly off-balance, a little afraid of what I might do next, I didn't want them to think I'd completely lost it.

My kids, to my surprise, did take the PI thing seriously.

I found this out when the boys came to me and asked for a conference. They sat me down in the living room. Jeff, at sixteen, was the spokesperson. Scott was eleven.

"Mom, we think it's really great that you're going to be a PI," he said. "It's great. We just have a few concerns."

I smiled to myself, because I recognized the conversational gambit. Whenever I had to say something to a kid that could be construed as negative, I would try to bracket it with something positive. As in, "Jeff, you're getting so tall and you're turning into such a handsome young man. Now, about that hair . . ."

"The thing is," he said, "we think it would be fair if you promised never to investigate *us*. I mean, if your mom was an investigator, would you want her to be following you around? Would you want to have to worry that she might read your e-mail?"

"So," I said, crossing my arms over my chest, "you're framing this as a privacy issue?"

Jeff thought for a moment. "How about a being-comfortable-in-your-own-house issue?"

"All right." I nodded. "I promise that I won't investigate you, Scott or

Christine, unless any of you show signs of drug use. I would consider that probable cause."

Jeff agreed. I was, on some level, flattered that they took me seriously.

Jay was encouraging, but he also had his own concerns. We were sitting on the back patio on a Sunday evening. The boys were watching TV and we were watching the sun go down. Jay went inside, got me a fresh Diet Coke and then handed it to me as he settled into the lawn chair with a sigh.

"Well?" I said.

"I think the PI thing is good. I'm glad you're going for it."

I nodded, waiting for the other shoe to drop.

"It suits your talents. It's a business that doesn't need a ton of inventory or start-up capital. I guess my one problem with it is that I don't want you in danger. I don't want to worry that something's going to happen to you."

"Nothing will happen to me." I waved his concern away and popped open the top of my can. Jay made me promise to be careful, but I finally convinced him he didn't need to worry. And once my family was on board, I was good to go.

I was still new in town, but Jan knew everyone, so she had a lot of contacts. We handed out business cards and put up flyers in Albertson's. The flyers looked quite official, I thought, with our formal business name—Hanady Investigations—and our business nickname, Two Moms in a Minivan. We listed the different sorts of investigations we offered—an impressive bulleted list that included cheating spouses, insurance fraud, wayward teens, lost loves, adoption searches, background checks, and more. Much more. It was a long list, and we hadn't done a single one of those things yet. Our saving grace was that we didn't charge anything.

One way and another, the word got out, and cases started to come our way. A lot of our early cases were favors for friends. A friend or acquaintance might approach us in church and say, "I think my husband's cheating. Could you check up on him for me?" We'd follow him to see what he was up to, after stocking the van with all the essentials—M&M's, Diet Coke, porta-potty, and maybe a book to read, because surveillance meant basically sitting in a car for hours, waiting for something to happen. Or sometimes, a spouse who suspected that his wife was cheating might bring us some of her underwear, which we'd test with a semen-detection product called CheckMate.

One Sunday, a woman I knew slightly from my Bible study class lingered after everyone else had left the room. I was being slow, because I'd dropped a three-ring binder that had popped open.

"Your kids seem nice," she said, sidling up to me. "They don't seem like they give you much trouble." She smiled. "They're still pretty young, aren't they?"

"Yes, they are," I said. I had a flash of intuition about where she was going with this, so I said, "They're too young to get in trouble, but I know that day will come. Every parent has to deal with issues at some point." I was giving her an opening.

"Someone told me that you do investigations," she said, leaning in toward me so no one would overhear. "I kind of need some help. I think maybe my kid is using drugs. He's got a new group of friends and I don't like them. His grades have gone off a cliff, so I just would like someone to follow him who knows what she's doing."

"We're learning as we go," I said, snapping the binder rings shut. "We're new to investigation, but we're happy to help as a favor. Does that work for you?"

"You mean you do it for free?" Her face brightened.

"If we send hair to a lab for analysis, you'd have to pay for that."

We didn't charge money, because we knew we weren't professionals yet, but it never was a hobby. I was serious about it from the moment I started.

The case was interesting. On the one hand, it turned out to be pretty straightforward. The woman knew that Ryan, her fourteen-year-old, was hanging out at Capitol Park in downtown Boise. I sat in a car across the street from the park the next Friday night and photographed her kid buying drugs.

I sent a lock of his hair to a lab to be analyzed. That was easy. Anyone can do it. All it takes is ninety or more hairs, cut close to the root, and a few hundred dollars. The traces of drugs collect in the follicle and become encased in the hair as it grows. An immunoassay found trace amounts of drug metabolites. The lab confirmed the results with the gold standard of drug tests, a gas chromatograph/mass spectrometer that definitively identifies molecular structure. Ryan's hair contained molecules of cocaine and pot.

The hard part was the intensity of Mom's reaction when her suspicions were confirmed. It was a circumstance we faced time and again as cases unfolded. It's one thing to suspect that something is wrong and a whole other thing to know for sure. In cheater cases, especially, the documentation could be pretty graphic. Sometimes we spent as much time counseling clients as we did investigating.

Jan and I had suspected from the beginning that our learning curve would be steep and that we would make some mistakes. We got that part right.

Early on, we attended a Chamber of Commerce lunch for start-up businesses. Afterward, we were approached by Sandra, a friend of Jan's, the wife of a prominent local businessman. She'd been having problems in her marriage, she said, and now she told Jan that her husband was moving out. Something was terribly wrong. She had to know what. Could we help her to find out?

We gave her our standard line at the time: We can't charge, but we'll do it as a favor. We were actually quite happy to oblige in this particular instance. Her husband was a legend-in-his-own-mind sort of guy, a pompous man who'd corner me at parties after a few drinks and talk about himself.

We stocked the minivan with candy, Coke, porta-potty and so on. Jan insisted on driving, like she always does. She would never say, "You're a terrible driver, you have no driving talent whatsoever, and riding with you is suicidal," even though that's what she means. Instead, she says, "Oh I'll pick you up, no problem. You're on the way."

Her minivan pulled up in front of my house at dusk. She'd brought along a few friends just to liven things up. We parked down the street from this man's big house in an upscale neighborhood. There was a full moon, so even with his yard lights off, he was clearly visible as he got into his Lexus. That was a break for us, we thought, because we'd brought the video camera. At that time, the video cameras we had were giant—they looked like news cameras, and they rested on our shoulders.

The tape opens with a half hour of footage of the back of his car—not only boring, but useless. Following a car is harder than TV makes it look. On TV people don't know they're being followed. In real life, you have to stay far enough back so that your subject doesn't notice you. Hit a red light and it's over, unless the road is straight forever.

We followed him through the outskirts of Boise. He drove west on

I-84, and we thought maybe he was headed toward Nampa, which has a reputation for being a tough town. Instead, he exited near Meridian and pulled into a storage rental place. We couldn't follow him in because there was a chain-link fence, but the place was well lit, and we could clearly observe his unit from a side access road. We set up the camera and started filming. He unlocked the unit and went inside. In the instant he had the door open, we saw a flash of what appeared to be racks of clothing.

Could he be fencing stolen merchandise? Living in the unit?

Soon the door opened, and out walked a woman in a cocktail dress and high heels. He was not a handsome guy, but she was no knockout either.

We were filming like crazy, but we didn't know that you're supposed to turn off the sound. Our evidence for the formal divorce proceedings featured a candid soundtrack, including such restrained, professional commentary as, "You go, girl," and "You're toast, sucker," followed by an off-key rendition of "Who Let the Dogs Out?"

I didn't know what I was doing, really, although the job got done— even if it was done in a silly, lucky way. The one thing we had going for us was that we knew we didn't know.

Once the case was resolved, though, we did something I wish we hadn't. We gossiped about it. We didn't use names, but it was pretty clear who we were talking about. I also recounted the story during a radio interview, and one of Sandra's friends happened to hear it and told her.

Then, wouldn't you know it, I ran into her at a social event a few weeks later, a Memorial Day barbecue sponsored by several of the Chamber merchants. I was there with my kids. It was a beautiful day, but hot, I recall. We were all a little concerned about the mayonnaise in the egg salad, so we had set up the buffet table in the shade. I was making my way down one side of the table, and there was Sandra on the other side, loading shish kebab onto a plate. I felt a little panicky wave of guilt. Sandra looked up and realized who it was. She froze, a skewer in her hand, her eyes locked with mine.

I tried to finesse the encounter with a breezy, "Oh, hi there. Nice to. . ." But before I could finish the sentence, Sandra—her eyes drilling into mine—hissed, "Not interested. You've said quite enough." She turned on her heel and stalked off, abandoning her plate of food. She actually got into her car and left.

It was a horrible moment. I suppose I was lucky she didn't run me through with the skewer.

We had justified talking about her case by telling ourselves we hadn't taken money, therefore there was no contractual relationship and no breach of confidentiality—but we knew that it was. I had violated her trust, which was even worse. I never did that again.

In another early case, we were hired to visit different music stores to see if sales personnel were selling mature-rated CDs to underage kids. The company we were working for was a contractor that businesses hired to check up on employees' behavior. If, for example, a store wanted to find out how their employees treated customers who were returning an item, they might hire this company to send a "shopper" to buy an item and then return it. In this case, the company wanted to know if the music store employees would break the rules and sell kids inappropriate adult music.

Jan and I hired Jesse, Jan's oldest boy, who was ten at the time, and my Scott, who was twelve, to be our shoppers. We gave them each fifty dollars to go into several music stores to buy a particular CD while Jan and I waited in the nearby snack bar. We were not so much sipping Cokes as keeping an eye on the boys. We were not about to put the kids in danger.

The first store sold the CD to them. So did the second. At the next store on our list, we sent Scott in by himself to pick up the CD. I was pretty sure that employees would think twice about letting an unaccompanied twelve-year-old child buy this CD all by himself. When Scott came out of the store clutching the disk with a smile on his face, I was just floored.

I decided to keep a copy and listen to it, because I was curious. *And really, how bad could it be?* I thought. The kids had no trouble getting copies. Turned out it was really horrible, completely and overtly sexual. Not even innuendo, just right out there. I couldn't believe they sold that stuff to young children, but we had proved they did.

Then I stepped over the line and went back to the store the next day to confront the clerk.

"What makes you think it's all right to break the law and sell that CD to a twelve-year-old?" I asked the salesclerk, who must have been all of nineteen himself. I leaned forward just a touch. "Are you the judge of what's appropriate?"

"Well, I . . . uh. . ." He took a step back. "I just assumed his mom would say it was okay."

"No," I said. "That's not what you're supposed to do. You're not supposed to assume anything about it." I held up the boxed disc, holding the thing by the corner as if I had a dead rat by the tail. "Here's the song I listened to. I think it would be good if you played it over the loudspeaker of your store. See how many of your customers who are here with children find it appropriate."

Fortunately, I remembered that we hadn't been hired to intervene. This was not our client's mandate to us—in any case, he was just the salesclerk. I didn't take it to the manager, which I otherwise would have done.

The next Sunday after church, we were all on a line to say good morning to Pastor Steve. As Pastor Steve took my hand, I heard Jesse's voice from somewhere behind us. "Guess what?" he said loudly. "My Aunt Valerie paid me to buy dirty music."

Despite that little bump in the road, our kids would play key roles in cases to come. Maybe it was inevitable because our lives were so entwined. They were our children and we were their moms—their spymoms.

Chapter 4
Cookies and a Hug

TWO MOMS IN A MINIVAN WERE WORKING CASES that were more fun than serious business, but it wasn't too long after the CD caper that we began to get some media attention.

We couldn't afford to advertise, but I thought that we might be able to get some free publicity if I could interest a magazine in doing a story about us. I wrote up a cover letter explaining that we were sisters who were private investigators and sent it off with a photograph. The slant was that we worked out of our homes, wrapping the spy business around family life. And, by the way, we were both cancer survivors.

I was thrilled when one of the very first magazines we approached, *Good Housekeeping*, decided to feature "Two Moms in a Minivan." Our story appeared in early September 2001. The story opened with a description of us filming an insurance fraud suspect in a grocery store. The piece called us the "snoop sisters" and described how we managed to "juggle carpooling with crime solving."

I was thrilled, but I had no idea what the impact of that one article would be.

As soon as the story appeared, people from my past began calling. People I hadn't seen in years wanted a favor or to trade services. And it wasn't confined to friends and acquaintances, either. Strangers who had picked up the magazine were calling. They'd say, "I read about you in my dentist's office." Or, "My mom clipped the article so I thought I would take a chance and call."

We were suddenly legitimate, because we were in a magazine. It was an early lesson about the power of media and encouraged me to keep sending material out.

However, our first truly serious case came to us not through media exposure, but from a personal contact. Jan heard from an old friend, some-one she liked a lot. The friend had a work acquaintance with a problem.

The acquaintance called Jan and said that her fourteen-year-old niece, Misty, had run away—or, as she believed, had been abducted by an older boyfriend. The family was frantic. They were afraid she was being held captive as his sex slave, that he had her tied up in a room somewhere. They had already contacted the police, who questioned the man and had evidently been convinced he had nothing to do with her disappearance. Misty's parents had taken to camping out in front of the boyfriend's house, waiting for him to come home or to leave so they could talk to him. They had approached him persistently enough to jus-tify his taking out a restraining order on *them*. The parents knew they had come to the end of the line. They couldn't keep chasing him around. But they didn't know what else to do.

That's when Misty's aunt called Jan. The family asked us to do sur-veillance on the boyfriend to determine whether he really did have her tied up in a back room.

So every morning I got the kids off to school, picked up Jan, drove through an espresso stand to get double mochas and then headed to the guy's house. We drove into a parking lot across the street and waited. Sure enough, at 8:40 every morning, he backed out of his driveway in his easy-to-follow white Trans Am with black hood stripes. We tailed him to the car lot where he was employed. He showed cars to as many as a dozen people in the course of a day. Then, every day, he took off his work jacket, got in his own car, and drove home.

"You know what," Jan said, as we were sitting there for the umpteenth hour of the umpteenth day. "This poor guy really has a—"

"really boring life." I nodded. That's the thing with sisters. We can finish each other's sentences.

"Look, look." She pointed to where our guy leaned on his porch rail. I adjusted the ridiculous granny wig I wore as a disguise and crouched down a little in the passenger seat.

"Why are you doing that?" Jan asked. "You know he can't see you."

"It's so clandestine," I said. "Jan, don't you ever feel like being a little . . . clandestine?"

"No."

Our subject had opened the garage door and was dragging his trash to the curb for Thursday pickup. I could hardly wait for him to go inside and go to bed so we could pick through his trash. We were new to the trash game and had no idea what we'd find.

"Wait," said Jan. "Put these on." She handed me a pair of yellow rubber gloves, like you wear to do dishes. She pulled on a pair.

"So what d'you think's the best approach here? Are we sneaky or are we just right out there?" I asked.

"When I repossess a car, I don't cringe or slink around. I just do it." She nodded.

"Jan, Jan, the repo man."

She gave me a withering look as she opened the car door. I watched her walk across the street, swinging her shoulders like she owned the block. She popped the top of his garbage can. Slowly and deliberately she withdrew the garbage bag and then sauntered back across the street. I was impressed. This was her turf, so to speak.

"Don't put that—"

"No, the trunk."

"You think he—"

"No, he doesn't, but it's—"

"Yeah, it could be."

By which we understood, in sibling shorthand, that the trash would not go on the car seat and that we would find no needles in the trash, although our fellow might be a pot smoker.

We went through it and found nothing more damning than coffee grounds and cat hair. Bravado aside, our skill level was such that anything more subtle than a crumpled note with: "Dear Diary, Today I tied little Misty to a chair," was likely to go unnoticed anyway.

Still, we came back every day and watched his house, and finally, we got our break. We were filing our nails and reading junk books—settled in for a long, uneventful Friday night, when boyface came tripping lightly down the front steps carrying a black box the size of a substantial suitcase. The size you have to check on an airline. The kind you can stuff a body into. He put the box into the trunk of his car and drove off into the night. We followed. We knew this was is it. Now something was going to happen.

He started driving faster than he had all week. He was whisking around corners, really zooming. Jan put the pedal to the metal. I think he must have known we were right behind him. I mean, we didn't have any finesse about tailing people yet. We would try to keep up and not be noticed, but Boise is a small enough place that it didn't take long for people to wonder, *Why is that van following me everywhere I go?*

"I'm turning off the camera," I said. "Let him think we're on the make. We're divorced, middle-aged women flirting with a cute guy."

"In a *minivan?*" Jan shook her head.

But Jan honked and we both waved. Just in case he was wondering.

He drove to a club, parked in the alley in the rear, unloaded the box and went in the back door. We went in the front, trying to act nonchalant. The next thing we knew, this guy's onstage as part of a band. The big black box was a speaker.

The upside was that the band was pretty good, so we stayed to line dance and had a night out.

By this point, we were pretty sure he was not involved in Misty's disappearance. We waited another few days to see if he would contact her, but he did not. He basically just went to work and came home.

We decided that if her disappearance wasn't due to foul play, she might well have run away. We had to hope she hadn't run far and that she hadn't run into any bad characters. Jan figured that if Misty was in the area, she had been able to exist fairly comfortably through the warm summer, but since it was now October and getting pretty cold, she was probably looking for a way to come home.

Jan really took on the case then. She started calling Misty's friends. These were teens, so they weren't much inclined to break ranks and tattle to an adult. Jan was careful. She said, "If there's any chance that you have contact with this girl, have her call her parents or have her call me. Work it out among yourselves how you want it to be, but just have

Misty call. Tell her I'm not picking sides or anything like that. I'm only appealing to her, as a mother myself, to at least let her own mother know that she's all right. That's all that her mother really wants. Just to know she's okay."

Finally, Jan got hold of a cousin that Misty was close to. The cousin told her that Misty had been staying with various friends, moving from one friend to the next when the parents asked her to leave. At last, she had run out of places to crash and was now living under a freeway overpass. Her circumstances had nothing to do with the boyfriend, with whom she was not even in contact.

The cousin went to the overpass and pled with Misty to just make contact. First the runaway spoke to Jan, who then persuaded her to call her parents. I doubt that Misty had any idea of what she had put her parents through or the massive relief they felt when they learned she was all right. Her mother was so grateful, she painted Jan's windows with Christmas scenes to welcome her home. The lady was a professional graphic artist, so her paintings were as good as the ones in store windows in downtown Boise.

We had found a missing person. We were on a roll. I began to think I knew a little something.

What was that about a little knowledge being a dangerous thing?

Jan and I were contacted by a woman who was a friend of Jan's neighbor. We met with Lori over breakfast at a Denny's near her house. She looked pitiful. Her blouse was stained and her jeans were dirty and her hair was every which way. She told us, between sobs, that her husband was cheating on her.

We were quite sympathetic because she was so torn up. I asked her what made her think so.

Lori picked her head up off the table. "Well, I know," she said, "because he's done it before."

"He has?" I laid down my fork. "Was there just one other time, then?"

"No," she said. "We've been married fourteen years and I think he's cheated every one of those years, throughout the marriage." Her husband was a salesman of some kind and was on the road a lot, so he had plenty of opportunity.

We established that Lori would give us a nine hundred dollar retainer to start. I asked her how many hours of surveillance she wanted us to do. I told her about the downside of surveillance—that Jan or I could sit there for hours, but nothing might happen.

She was determined to get at the truth, she said. She wanted to know if he was seeing someone and who that someone was. She wanted us to do whatever it took.

She seemed like someone who had finally had enough; she really wanted to take an unflinching look at the facts instead of just being fearful and suspicious.

If I'd known what she was going to do with the information, I never would have helped her find out who the other woman was.

Lori got us copies of her husband's phone records and we went through them number by number. By now Jan and I were using some professional databases. We paid a small fee to access a good reverse directory—the kind police and detectives have used for the last forty years. There are free ones online, but they're not as complete. They do not, for example, trace the unlisted numbers.

Once we had found names and addresses, we reduced the list to the names we thought were potentials. This process of elimination had as much to do with common sense as anything else. Obviously the sixty-five-year-old secretary at the dentist's office was not our gal. We were looking for home phone numbers. Women's names, or possibly couples, because she might be married.

Once we had it down to about six possible names and addresses, we followed him to see if he went to any of those locations. We finally did catch his truck in front of a woman's house. The next day, when we knew he was at work, I used a specialized digital connection to the telephone company—the ISDN PRI circuit—that enables private investigators to display a phone number other than the number from which the call is being placed. I set it to indicate the caller ID of a local hospital. By 2004, we'd be using the new "telespoof" card that lets the user punch in any caller ID once the card is activated by dialing a toll-free number. In 2006, there were Internet phone services that let users set any number as the caller ID. But in 2000, the process was still expensive and cumbersome.

I called the woman and told her that our man was in the hospital. We said she was listed as this man's contact person, but I couldn't release information to her without some identifying information: her name, phone number and social security number would do, for starters.

She was so worried, she told me all about herself and about her extended family too—everything I asked. Her name was Marci Stark and she had met Ronald at a club. We gathered a lengthy bio that we turned over to Lori. Then Lori did something unthinkable. She started calling the relatives of this lady—all the people related to the sweetheart—saying, for example, "Your daughter's ruining my marriage. She's carrying on with my husband and ruining the lives of my children."

It turned out that Lori had wanted to know who the woman was just so she could go after her to destroy her life, as she felt hers had been destroyed. After a while, I found myself sympathizing with the people she was calling. We had assumed that if Lori found out for an absolute fact that her husband was cheating on her, she would use the information to springboard out of the marriage. We were totally shocked when she took him back and started harassing all those people.

Jan and I sat with her and counseled her. "What good is this going to do?" I asked. "Harassing her isn't going to solve anything. The right way to handle this is to talk to your husband and put a stop to this. By behaving this way, you're just setting yourself up for it to happen again."

"Sure, this woman shouldn't be messing around with a married man," Jan chimed in, "but you don't know all the circumstances that might have driven her to it."

Lori owed us one more payment. She called and asked if we'd meet her at Chandlers Steakhouse. She wanted to buy us dinner to say thank you. Jan begged off. I wasn't really up for it, but I went. I thought we stood a better chance of getting paid if I picked up that last check.

Lori beat me there. I think she had gotten there early to have a wee drink or two.

"You guys," she said, rising to hug me. "I love you guys. You did such a great job. Of all the PIs down through the years, you were the best. Really."

She was effusive. I could not understand it. We had proved that she had been wronged once again, and she was in heaven.

She ordered steak and I ordered a grilled cheese sandwich and fries. While we waited for the food, she told me about the women he'd cheated with over the years.

"The first time, it was with a friend of mine. She was a teacher and I got her fired. I laid it out at a school board meeting. That was . . . 1987,

I think. Sophie was the next one—we were in Shreveport by then. Yeah, Shreveport. So that had to be 1989. She was the kids' babysitter. She was sixteen, but that's not statutory, there. I got into it with her back of Piggly-Wiggly. So now we're up to 1990. That was the first married one. I knew they had to have a place they were meeting, but I couldn't find it for anything until I hired a PI. That worked out great too. I got to break the news to her husband."

I had the oddest feeling. It was as if she were showing me her photo album and reminiscing. Then I got it. I finally, finally got it. This was her habitual response to his affairs. Each time it happened, she got someone to tell her who it was and then she went after them and their families. The attack was the payoff for her. This was what the marriage was about. They both got something out of it.

I cut off her little walk down memory lane. I told her, "Don't you dare ever call us again to look up anyone. I don't care how much you're going to pay us."

After Lori, we were no longer just the medium to funnel information to our clients. We were more selective. We learned to open cheater cases by asking the crunch question. At a first meeting, before we had a contract, I would ask them, "Have you thought about what you're going to do if I find out that he is cheating? Because if all you're going to do is take him back into your life, then you don't need me. But if you're going to take this information and put it to use—perhaps go to counseling and get some help—or if you're at least serious about making him move out until issues are worked out, then we'll do it."

Sometimes we would tell clients to go talk to an attorney and find out if they were assured of getting custody before we did anything.

When I first started out, I didn't believe that it mattered how someone used the information I gathered. All that was important was that I collect it and turn it over to them. That was all my job was, I thought. Very soon I learned to pay close attention to the motivation of the prospective client, and not just in cheater cases. There were times when a case opened with a background check of the client. We started to do due diligence to be certain we weren't helping a stalker find his quarry or an abusive spouse locate a hidden mate. I'm happy that we did not have to learn that one by trial and error.

The truth was, we had learned an enormous amount in a relatively short time. As our first year of investigating came to a close, I was grateful that a year that had had a rocky start was closing on a happy note, both professionally and personally.

Most of all, I was happy to put cancer behind me. It had served me well as a catalyst for change, and I could feel proud about what I had accomplished in its wake.

Chapter 5
Wallpaper and Grass

TWO MOMS IN A MINIVAN—OR, MORE FORMALLY, Hanady Investigations—was already doing better than I had imagined it would. Following our exposure in *Good Housekeeping, The Idaho Statesman* approached us for what would be the first of many articles featuring Two Moms.

Jan and I were now not the rank beginners we had been just twelve months before. We knew how to do basic surveillance and basic research. We were now charging clients and that was a big deal. The only problem was that we each made about twelve dollars an hour and I was ready to make more. I was also ready to learn more.

That's when I ran across an ad in our local paper, placed by an insurance company based in North Carolina. They were looking for an investigator to work their insurance fraud cases in Idaho. The company would fly the new hire to North Carolina for ten days of training in investigative techniques. That person would then come back to Idaho and work for them. It seemed like a really good way to get some formal training.

I answered the ad and they hired me. Jay was supportive and the kids thought it was kind of a cool thing for Mom to do. I would train in North Carolina and then I would be able to show Jan what they had taught me. We would both benefit because we could then bill an hour's work at fifty dollars. Jan and I could split that. That was the plan.

There would also be benefits that I couldn't have foreseen: a push to find my own creative ways to investigate and a delightful new partnership with my dad.

I flew to North Carolina for ten days of intensive training at corporate headquarters. I was part of a class of about twenty students from all over the United States. There was only one other woman in the group and she had been a police officer.

We learned by working through sample cases. They'd pass out copies of the investigator's report on a situation and we would go over it in class. A lot of what we learned was about keeping good records of our surveillance, keeping track of where we went and when, and learning how to write a thorough report of what we had observed. There was a big emphasis on photo documentation and video evidence.

They always emphasized "getting the shot." That was the important thing. To prove someone guilty of insurance fraud, you had to establish their identity and you had to show your subjects engaged in physical activity that proved they weren't impaired as they had claimed. When you know you can get that picture, they emphasized, go ahead and do whatever it takes to get the shot.

This company also had their own version of what was ethical and what was not. You could not, for example, photograph someone inside his home. That was the company's rule, not a legal issue, and since a lot of bad behavior happens behind closed doors, that was frustrating. At least North Carolina and Idaho are not among the states that flat-out forbid the unauthorized use of cameras on private land. If your subject posts a No Trespassing sign on the property, you're supposed to stay out. No sign, you're good to go.

There was hands-on learning too. We went into the field to see first-hand what information they wanted us to gather. We wrote case reports and executed proper case management. It was basically insurance boot camp, but it was also a lot of fun. Besides hanging out with my fellow students, I got to know the women working in the office, and even helped plan a birthday party for one of them. In turn, they presented me with a T-shirt with my name and "Graduate of the Class of 2001."

I came home ready to take on the world. They were ready to hand it to me too. I was to be this company's sole representative for the whole state of Idaho. I realized they had no idea about Idaho's geography or what "big" means on the Western scale when they kept trying to send me to Coeur d'Alene for the day. That's about eleven hours of driving. These people in their modest-sized East Coast state were thinking Delaware when they should have been thinking Texas.

In any case, I had told them that I could only cover the territory I could reach between dropping kids off at school and dinnertime. Their interpretation of that was to have me work six to six. Still, they had trained me, so I gave them a year. By the time that year was up, I could photograph anybody any time, any place, anywhere. I felt completely comfortable doing surveillance.

Unfortunately, it didn't take me a year to learn to dislike it. Traditional surveillance is boring. It's either really hot or really cold, and there are no toilet facilities. I couldn't even pee in pop bottle like the guys.

I spent hours crouching behind some bushes or trying to stay awake in my car waiting for some guy supposedly confined to a wheelchair to forget himself and walk. I got so bored I would imagine entire production numbers. My subject would fling open the front door and tap-dance down the front walk like Fred Astaire, in top hat and tails, with his girlfriend, transformed into Ginger Rogers. I would film them both and rewrite PI history.

The gritty truth was, as conventionally practiced, surveillance was pretty much a mundane job. And while I was making steady money, the company's methods were inefficient. All those hours of passive surveillance could be condensed, I thought, with a little ingenuity.

A woman I was assigned to investigate was receiving disability for an injury that supposedly kept her from raising her arms or using her hands. She kept horses, and the company was hoping to catch her out pitching hay or brushing a horse. They told me to park at a construction site above her house and to tape her horse paddock every hour on the hour, whether anything was happening or not, starting at 6:00 AM. So I did twelve hours of this, day after day.

After a week of twelve-hour days, packed with absolutely nothing, I got an idea. I did a little independent investigating and found out that she taught classes at a local beauty college. I called the school and said I was calling on behalf of my daughter, who wanted to study cosmetology. And the thing was, since I was paying for the course, I wanted to make sure that the instruction was hands-on.

Oh yes, they said. It was totally hands-on, and the instructors got right in there and demonstrated every technique and worked right alongside the students.

I photographed my subject walking in the door to teach these hands-on classes, but the insurance company wanted nothing to do with this.

Even though she was listed in the beauty school catalog as an instructor, and even though I could document that she had to use her hands and arms while teaching, they could not see beyond their tried-and-true methodology. They preferred me to work for twelve hours at something I could have accomplished in two.

Somewhere inside me, a decision to go my own way was forming.

After three months of back-to-back twelve-hour days, I overslept one morning. If I couldn't get to the horse paddock by six, I'd have to manipulate the time on the camera or lose a whole day. I called my dad and asked him if he'd do me a giant favor and go to the site and start the surveillance for me.

At about seven o'clock, I pulled up next to Dad's car. He was so concentrated on watching for action at the horse paddock that he didn't even notice me at first. He had brought his binoculars and he had them trained on our subject. She was puttering around below the paddock. Dad had his window rolled down and I could hear him coaching her to slip up.

"C'mon, lady," he said. "Pick up that trash can. You know you want to. Just carry it a few feet, that's all I need. You have a trashy yard, why don't you get your clippers and trim a few hedges. Be a doll and load up that wheelbarrow. That'd do it. That'd fix you right up."

"Hi," I said. "How's it going?"

"You know this is *fun*," he said, handing me the binoculars. "You can ask me to do this any time."

"Well, then, I have an idea," I said. "If you felt like it, you could go and

get us some sodas and keep me company. Because I find this unbelievably boring to do by myself."

"You think?" He said. "I kind of like it. People are interesting."

He did return, and he stayed with me on and off throughout that
day and the next. We took turns looking through the binoculars, and we
laughed at the silly things people do when they think they are alone and
unobserved. We made bets on what she'd do next, and even on when
she'd come out of the house and go back in.

It was a blast, sharing that with my dad. His presence completely
transformed the experience.

That was the beginning of his involvement with my cases. The father
who'd been a little remote and a tough disciplinarian had already mel-
lowed into something of a friend. Now, he became my confidant. He
loved it that I was working as a PI and cheered me on. He took delight in
hearing about our adventures and followed each case in detail. Soon, he
was even collaborating. It started when I was complaining one day about
the difficulty of getting inside the house to document what was happening for a cheater case.

"Why do you need to personally go in?" he said. "Why can't you plant
a device to do your spying for you? I could make you something that
could be carried in. Something they'd never suspect."

I still have that first item he made for us. I had bought a tiny pinhole
camera, and he drilled a hole in a plant basket and fit the aperture of the
camera to the hole. This was before digital, so he'd rigged it to be battery-
powered. We got it delivered to a cheater gal and we got lucky because
she put the thing on the coffee table in front of the couch where a significant part of the action took place. Thanks, little cheater gal.

Thanks, Dad.

A retired engineer who could make or fix anything, Dad got a terrific charge from creating a range of unique spy devices for us. He even built a special room in the garage, a workshop devoted to our projects. He took real pride in his work and wouldn't let us see a project until he had it all set up. He was very creative in finding ingenious places for the little cameras.

Once, Dad made a giant stuffed bunny and had inserted minicams at different levels. The retooled rabbit could be set up as part of a store display to catch shoplifters or monitor employees. The bunny was his personal favorite and he'd challenge visitors to find the cameras.

Most of our collaboration began with a question. "So what's the latest?" he might say. "Update me on the latest, greatest PI doings." He'd ask for details, and not just from casual curiosity—although he did find the cases interesting that way too. As I told him about what we were working on, his engineering mind was sorting and classifying all the information that he would later bring to bear on the technological solution.

He made teddy bears for kids to carry on a visit to parents in a custody case. While we never saw or recorded anything definitive, the evidence that there was no abuse was reassuring to clients. He camouflaged one camera that absolutely had to be plugged in by hiding it in a string of Christmas lights.

Once, when my sister Vickie's daughter, Asali, suspected a neighbor of abusing her cat, Dad made her a birdhouse with a fish-eye lens in the opening. He located the tall birdhouse strategically to overlook the offending neighbor's yard.

I loved sharing being a PI with him. For so much of my childhood he'd been revered, but remote. We played board games as a family when I was young and we had gone camping as a family, but there hadn't been that one-on-one time. Even now, we did things as couples—Jay and I with Dad and Mom. But working with Dad on Hanady was a chance for us to know each other as individuals. He was the one I could run to and say, "Oh, we have a story in *The Idaho Statesman*" or "I've got this funny case, let me tell you about it." It was something between us that was special. Except for Jan, I really didn't talk about cases to anyone but Dad.

I loved walking up to his workshop at dusk. I often found him at a workbench, bent over some project or other. I'd pull up a stool and, while he tinkered, conversation meandered this way and that, with an ease we couldn't have when he was the strict dad and I was the know-it-all kid. If he was a little tired and seemed more often under the weather, we found it easy to write it off to aging. He didn't make much of it, so we didn't either.

Our cases were becoming more interesting. I was branching out and finding my own way as a PI, even though Jan and I didn't always agree about where the boundaries lay between what was acceptable and what was not. Jan is not only a tough repo gal, she is also tough in a moral sense—very tuned into the finer points of right and wrong. It didn't take long for her to begin to sift through potential cases looking for moral quicksand.

I was comfortable with pretexting—assuming a role in order to beguile investigative subjects into revealing information. To Jan, representing herself as something she is not in order to get information is a lie. She doesn't have a problem repossessing someone's car or collecting on a bad loan, and she would call anyone and ask them anything—but only as herself.

I'm a terrible liar, but to me, pretexting is acting. Almost all PIs use the pretext, but mostly on the phone. I was finding I could make up a story in person, on the spot.

I had come to love acting a part after buying into Death by Murder. Once the year of working for the insurance company was done, I'd gotten more involved in acting with the company. I really got into a role, and the more different from me the character was, the better. I took a night off from being Valerie to become a ghost, a countess, a vampire, or a queen. We didn't learn lines, we just inhabited a character. I could dress outrageously and be as over the top as I wanted.

Now, I found that creating a PI pretext was playing a part, like improv theater. You had to be completely focused and stay on top of the situation in order to respond instantaneously. It sometimes seemed like an incredibly intense game of ping-pong.

I found that pretexting was not only fun, but effective. If I wanted to spend my client's money to maximum effect, I could get a lot more done if I knocked on the door on some pretext than if I sat out in front of the house and waited to see whether they went to the grocery store or not.

When I began to branch out into taking insurance fraud cases for other companies, I found that the pretext approach was welcomed.

Once, we were investigating a young man who claimed to have sustained a disabling back injury in a minor fender bender. He could not, he said, bend to tie his shoes or even carry his trash to the bin behind his apartment building.

I sat out front and waited and waited for him to do something physical that we could get on tape. I drank four thousand Diet Cokes. My feet kept falling asleep, to say nothing of my behind. Finally I decided that this was ridiculous. I bought two huge bags of soil from the home and garden store and put them in the back of my pickup. I parked over by this huge iron fence in front of the apartment complex. I went and knocked on his door and said, "Hi, I know this sounds silly, but is there anyone who could help me throw these bags of dirt over the fence? I'm the landscape architect for the apartment complex. I expected workers here, they're not here. I have to start. Would you do that for me?"

"Sure." He smiled at me.

He immediately picked up the bags and threw them over the fence before I could get the video cameras going. I was so mad.

So I said, "Gee, that's nice. But you know what? I've got two more bags. Would you throw them over the fence, too, if I bring them here? I'd actually pay you for it."

"Absolutely," he said, none the wiser.

So I drove around the corner and picked up the same two bags. Dragged them, actually, they were so heavy. I knocked on his door again.

"Don't throw them over until I videotape you," I said, smiling as innocently as I could. "Because if I don't tape you doing this work and getting paid, I can't prove to my employers I paid someone and I won't be reimbursed."

He bought it. When the tape was rolling and he was ready, I talked to the camera, pretended to record the event for my employer. "See, Mr. Jones?" I said. "I'm having to pay someone to throw this over the fence. This huge, eight-foot fence."

I turned to the suspect. "Now be sure you don't hurt yourself, because I know how heavy it was when I tried to move it to the back of the pickup. Does that hurt you at all?"

"No, not a bit." He hoisted the first bag onto his shoulder and over his fence.

"If it hurts you the tiniest bit, you stop right now," I said, trying not to laugh. "Because I don't want to be sued."

"No," he said. "Really. It's fine." And to show how fine he was, he lifted the second bag high over his head and heaved it right over the fence.

We brought the tape to the attorney. In fact, attorneys from all the other offices in the building came for the grand premiere. They could not believe it. They thought it was the funniest thing.

That young man and I had spent at least twenty minutes in each other's company, with lots of face-to-face interaction, but when I went to court to testify, he walked right by me without a sign of recognition. Several times. He didn't even remember me. That hurt.

But I think this case might have been the first time I realized I had what amounted to a superpower—a cloak of invisibility. As middle-aged women, we're basically invisible. No one notices us. We're like grass, like wallpaper. I think, sometimes, that I could go through windows or walls, maybe. I'm that kind of invisible.

I can't say that I was immediately thrilled to the core when I realized that I could go places and not be noticed. I wanted to be a super-sexy spy babe just *disguised* as a middle-aged mom. Still, as a PI, I would learn to use it to my advantage. As a middle-aged mother I was always under-cover. I could go anywhere and no one would look twice.

Jan and I would take video cameras into the bars or wherever we happened to find our subjects. We would shoot footage or take pictures of ourselves with the subjects in the background. Sometimes we'd actually get them to pose with us. We could do whatever we wanted, we could be as bold as we dared, because no one remembered what we looked like. That realization was a turning point.

Chapter 6
Sister Sister

PEOPLE SEEMED INTERESTED IN TWO MOMS IN A MINIVAN.
Requests for interviews were steady. We were featured in *Entrepreneur*
and *Home Business*. One of the local radio stations even interviewed
Dad for his growing role as our official f/x man. I'd thought that Jan
would be as happy as I was about all the media attention, but I was way
off. She did not like being in the spotlight. Not at all.

In fact, she hated every minute of it.

When I got us placed in *More*, a well-regarded magazine for middle-
aged women, Jan complained that I'd put us in an "old lady magazine."
Even the serious articles in magazines like *Good Housekeeping* made her
uneasy. She didn't want to be perceived as goofy. She was afraid I would
make us seem that way. The fact is, not only can I be goofy and silly, I
have a real appreciation for those attributes.

We were invited to be on *The Deborah Duncan Show*, a Houston-
based TV talk show. We knew they wanted to talk to us about being
PI moms, but we didn't have any idea of what the overall theme of the
whole show would be.

They flew us to Texas and wined and dined us. We washed down mustard-crusted spareribs with ale from a local microbrewery. Our hotel room had a Jacuzzi and a panoramic view of the city. That part was fabulous. It was only in the green room, a sort of holding pen where guests wait to go onstage, that we found out that the theme of the show was women with unusual occupations.

"Unusual" didn't set off alarm bells for me. We met some of the other guests. They seemed okay. Then we asked one very put-together woman what she did, and she said, quite matter-of-factly, "Oh, I test adult toys for a living." She held up a pair of filmy panties. "Cinnamon swirl," she said.

I could feel Jan, who was just behind me, begin to seethe. I did not have to turn around to know what her expression was.

The encounter was cut short by the producer, who popped into the room to pass out costumes to various guests. He handed several items to Jan and to me. I got a pair of dark glasses and a fedora, which were all right.

Jan, however, had to wear a trench coat. It was about four thousand degrees in Houston and she was sweating without a coat. It was pretty awful. Also, the trench coat was way too small. The sleeves ended at her elbows. The hemline was well above her knees, while her suit skirt came to mid-calf. She'd spent a small fortune on a new suit to look good on TV and now the effect was totally ruined. Being forced to wear too-small clothing on TV was not her idea of a good time.

For the introduction, they filmed us crawling through underbrush and holding up spyglasses and peering at stuff with a magnifying glass. All of that was, of course, about as goofy as it gets. Jan just hated it.

Then we were supposed to be on next, and Jan kept muttering, "I'm not going to do this." I kept hissing at her, "You're *going* to do it," and then the guy just pushed us out there. We went onstage to be interviewed, and I had walked on first so I sat down, but it turned out to be the wrong chair. Jan had followed me on and we wound up sort of dancing around each other for a bit. For someone who doesn't like "silly," it had to be a whole bunch of awful.

As we left, they gave her a copy of the tape, but no family member has ever viewed the thing. Jan says she's never watched it. She would rather, she says, poke out her eyes.

That interview was really the beginning of the end for Jan.

Then, cancer really put an end to our PI partnership.

Every six months, I would have a mammogram—at my insistence, because insurance would only pay for one a year. I was due for one again. It was fall; October of 2003. Three years had passed since my cancer diagnosis.

I wasn't worried about the mammogram. My biggest problem was that I'd always found the mammogram clinic to be overly enthusiastic about the color pink. As I waited for the test, did I really need to be staring at pink walls from my blue and pink-striped chair, while clutching my pink print, front-opening mammography gown so my remaining pink breast would not play peek-a-boo? Didn't they know that all the pinkness just made the mean green masher machine seem cold and hard by comparison?

That afternoon, I put that part of my anatomy through the proverbial wringer and was then dismissed to dress. I zipped, buttoned and slipped back into shoes, I slung my purse over my shoulder—I was that close to escape—when the nurse rustled the curtain and said, sotto voce, "Doctor needs to see you, dear."

I sat down. They had found a tiny bit of cancer in my left breast. This tumor was much smaller than the first one. They did an ultrasound and went through the whole bit all over again. This time the news was good. It had not spread to the lymph nodes.

I'd been down this road before. I knew the drill. It was more of an annoyance than anything. I had another mastectomy so there would be no place for breast cancer to take hold again.

I had radiation and I took some of the newer drugs. Since the cancer hadn't spread, and since I didn't want to lose my hair again and gain weight, I decided not to have the most intense chemotherapy. I talked them out of giving me Benadryl this time, and it was great not to be zonked out on that stuff. I really didn't need it, because I did not have a bad reaction to the drugs.

Everyone was so worried about poor Valerie. They took care of me and loved me and brought me soup. Baked me cookies.

Then my dang little sister went and got breast cancer three weeks later. She found her own lump and was diagnosed in November.

"You're just doing this because I have cancer again," I accused her. "Couldn't you have waited just a year or even just a month, so I could have enjoyed the sympathy a bit longer?" I was kidding—sort of.

Jan's joke, when she was first diagnosed in 1995, had been that since the chances for women with our family's cancer history were one in three, she was the one in three. Vickie and I would be spared and we owed her. Then, when I was first diagnosed, Jan told the family I couldn't stand to have her outdo me. Then I pulled ahead of her with a second diagnosis, so she just had to catch up.

Irony and humor aside, both Jan and I had always been aware that we were at risk for cancer, in light of our family's breast cancer history. To us, it was just a question of when, and at what stage it would be discovered. Even so, it was shocking that both of us had been diagnosed within three weeks of each other.

I recalled the genetic test that I had passed up. Now, I pushed to have that test. My doctor did not suggest it. I had to take the initiative. I wanted to know the truth. I was tested and Jan was too. Samples of our blood were sent for analysis to a lab in Salt Lake City. When our results came back, we learned that both of us have genetic damage that promotes certain cancers.

Women with the BRCA1 mutation have a high risk of getting breast cancer at a young age. A particular protein on BRCA1 usually repairs mutations that occur in other genes. On a mutated BRCA1 gene, however, that protein is too short to do the job, so damaged genes accumulate. When enough have accrued, cancer is likely. Over the course of our lifetimes, Jan and I had a ninety percent chance of getting breast cancer. We were vulnerable to cancer. Our protective shields were down.

The good news was that our test results could serve as a baseline for other family members. Our known mutation could be compared to their DNA to give them an indication of their risk. To me, that was the most important reason to be tested. My kids would be able to test to see whether they were at increased risk for breast and ovarian cancer. Christine did get tested and she did not have the BRCA1 alteration. Her breast cancer risk is no greater than most people's, and that's a wonderful thing to know. The test applied to the boys, too, because BRCA1 damage meant a higher incidence of colon and prostate cancers. Although they chose not to test now, the results would be on file if they decided to test when they were older or when they had children.

The stress of Cancer, the Sequel was proving tough on both boys. While I was distracted with chemo, they found an outlet in mischief.

One of Jeff's friends bought some weed and Jeff picked up the bag for him. When the friend got caught, he claimed that Jeff had set up the whole deal.

Then Scott and his buddies decided to build a tiny bomb. They hollowed out a tennis ball, filled it with matches and set it on fire in the driveway of a friend's house. But Scott had told everyone at school about their project and he'd also kept careful notes about how to improve the device—notes that were retrieved from his back pocket by school officials.

My kids' "projects" came to light shortly after the Columbine shootings. The Christian school decided that both the school and my sons might mutually benefit from the boys' relocation to another educational setting. Jeff sealed his fate by saying "Thanks, but no thanks" to an invitation to beg forgiveness from school administrators. He would, he told them, prefer to take the matter up with God.

When life was difficult for my sons, my dad stepped in. He took them on rock-finding expeditions and showed them how to polish the stones. He took each of them fishing and on trips into the mountains on bikes or ATVs. He wanted to help them and protect me. He told them, "Tell me anything you want to or yell at me—anything you want to yell. You're free to say and do anything you need to with me."

When Jan started chemotherapy, Dad stepped up—along with my mother, who could always be counted on to show unconditional love in any crisis—to help her out too. Jan's kids were younger than mine, and soon my parents' cars were filled with baseball gloves, bike helmets and the odd knee pad. They joked that they were the only ones among their group of friends who still carted around kid paraphernalia.

Jan needed the help because she didn't tolerate chemo well. She was flattened by nausea two weeks out of every four. She had passed up the radiation, but had opted for the harshest, heavy-duty chemotherapy. She told her doctor to just go for it. She was tired of this and didn't want to deal with it again.

She lost her hair and gained weight. My experience was very different from Jan's and not just because I tolerated chemo better. We were being treated by different doctors and at different hospitals. Her treatment was more intense. I was tired and my digestive system was out of whack, but I felt basically okay.

A few days before Christmas, I went to see Dad. We usually talked about what new cases entailed so he could tailor the listening device to the unique circumstances. But this particular day, he must have read my body language, which wouldn't have been too hard, as I practically crawled up the driveway to the garage.

"Pull up a chair, Valerie Ann," he said, pointing to the stool. "You look like you could use a little early Christmas." He plucked a package down from a high shelf. "I made you this," he said, handing me a wooden box about six inches square with intricate Celtic knots carved into the lid and sides. The box alone would have been a breathtaking gift.

Since Dad had become something of a rock hound, I'd often admired his collection. Now, I opened the box to see a smooth stone nestled in sweet-smelling cedar shavings.

I opened an envelope that had been half-hidden in the shavings. I read: "This talisman is to protect you from cancer forever and ever. Keep hold of it and don't lose it, and you will be safe." I was incredibly moved.

Too soon I realized it was as much for him as it was for me. As it turned out, Dad needed his own talisman. He was sick. Doctors had finally figured out that his fatigue was an underlying symptom of a serious condition. They had diagnosed him with leukemia. There was no specific treatment, they said.

I tried not to think about what that meant.

I wasn't thinking very clearly. Irrationally, I felt deserted by the medical establishment because I wasn't doing the infusions that would have put me in the care of the chemo nurses. This time, when I was done at the hospital, they just sent me home to take my pills. I was very much at loose ends.

It's true that there was more support, in general, for women with breast cancer than there had been when I was first diagnosed in 1999. People were talking about breast cancer more openly. It was on the news. Still, improvements in the social climate weren't enough to keep me from feeling alone. I felt left out because Jan was getting all the attention. I knew this wasn't a nice thing to feel, especially because Jan was a fantastic sister and friend, and I deeply appreciated having her in my life, but I did feel that way.

I wound up doing everyone's Christmas shopping and resented it. Two days before Christmas, I walked for miles and miles in the mall as I was trying to finish up. I wanted to find something for Vickie. I thought maybe I'd be inspired by Macy's Christmas displays.

I was between the cosmetic counter and the shoe department, when it hit me. Over the store sound track I heard Judy Garland singing "Have Yourself a Merry Little Christmas" and I just lost it. I don't mean I shed a few discrete tears. I'm talking full-on sobbing that sends your mascara south. Underneath their dang bright lights. I was exasperated with myself and with cancer and the holidays.

Salesclerks emerged from behind the Lancôme and Clinique counters and converged on distraught, middle-aged me. Perfectly coifed and made-up women were waving tissues like little flags of truce. I knew they meant well, and I appreciated it, but let's face it, this was not a shining moment for *moi*.

I did the only thing I could. I held up my hand authoritatively in the "stop" gesture of cops and crossing guards.

They hesitated, uncertain, giving me a chance to regroup. I gathered my bags, bundles, boxes and purse, and when I had everything more or less in hand, I walked toward the nearest exit, head held high.

After Jan was re-diagnosed, she decided she couldn't handle doing PI work while undergoing a year of chemotherapy and reconstructive surgery. She needed to focus completely on getting healthy, she said. She quit all her church work too. She told everyone, "Call me in a year if I'm still hanging in."

Jan had worked with me for close to three years—into late 2003. Sometimes she was enthusiastic about Two Moms in a Minivan. Most often it seemed that she was keeping me company and being support-ive. When all was said and done, being a PI wasn't really her sort of thing, but I did appreciate our time together. We had loads of fun and we learned a lot. With Jan, I grew from amateur sleuth to professional investigator. I knew that she was doing what she needed to do. As far as Hanady was concerned, Jan had moved on.

Death by Murder was basically over too. I was too busy recruiting actors and producing the shows to act in them, which was the fun part. I could feel myself disengaging.

And Dad was leaving us. It didn't seem possible that he wouldn't be there to share in the fun of Hanady or to watch his grandchildren grow. It didn't seem possible, but I knew that it was coming.

Everything was changing. I was on my own.

Chapter 7
Enter Spymoms

IN THE SUMMER OF 2004, TWO MOMS IN A MINIVAN was invited to appear on the *Today* show in New York City. I had sent off a cover letter without really expecting any response. Almost immediately they got in touch, wanting us to be on the show. The *Today* show would give our tiny local business national exposure. There was no question of not doing it.

The problem was that they wanted Two Moms in a Minivan. Jan refused to do it, and it would be lamer than lame to have one lonely mom rattling around in a minivan. I needed someone to appear on the show with me, but I had no idea how I'd find a new partner with less than two weeks to go before taping.

I was turning over this problem as Jay and I drove to an evening of auditions for Death by Murder. We were going to watch the casting of the newest production. It would be a romp about murder in the Old West, with gamblers, cowboys, prospectors and saloon gals galore. I was a little wistful thinking about how much fun it would have been to participate.

I put a good face on it as I took a seat on the sidelines and waited for the auditions to start. A woman sitting next to me immediately introduced herself as Mollie. Most people would have given me a quick glance and nod, but Mollie turned around in her seat to fully engage me.

I wasn't sure how old she was. She looked like she could have been in her early forties. She was thin and blonde. Pretty. Put her in an oversized sweatshirt and a baseball cap with the brim turned backward, and she could have passed for mid-twenties.

"I'm new to Boise. We moved here about a year ago," she said. "I read about the audition in the paper and I said to myself, 'Oh, that's fun.'"

"It is, it's a lot of fun," I said. "I'm actually a co-owner. You'll like it, and you can earn money. Not much, but something."

"I was a gymnastics instructor for seven years in Milwaukee. I want to make some extra money, but because of my condition I can't, like, go somewhere and get a job and guarantee them that I'll be there and be on my feet for eight hours at a time."

"Ah." I nodded. I understood that situation. "Is it all right to ask what you have?"

"That's fine. I have psoriatic spondylitis," she answered. "It's an auto-immune disease, as in, my immune system misfires and attacks my body in any organ or joint. I have a fused sacrum and a deteriorating spine, among other things. Sometimes I feel more at home with my mom's seventy-year-old friends than people my own age. Her friends talk about the latest shot they got for pain, and I'm, like, 'I want a shot.'"

I laughed. "I'm a breast cancer survivor," I said. "My sister too."

"That's a rough road. Four of my friends are survivors," Mollie said, "and my mother just finished chemo. I have the pink ribbon tattooed over my heart. Oh, I'm sorry. What's your name?"

"Valerie." I held out my hand.

"No kidding. My mother's name is Valerie. Valerie Ann."

"Oh my gosh." We stared at each other. "My middle name is also Ann. Valerie Ann." The coincidence gave me goose bumps.

"This is too weird." She leaned forward in her chair. "What else do you do?"

"I have three kids and I'm a private investigator."

Mollie's jaw literally dropped. "You're not those two sisters I read about in *Good Housekeeping* magazine, are you?"

"That's me. Well, I mean, obviously I'm just one of them."

"No way," she said, her voice rising an octave. "No way. I can't believe I'm meeting you. You're incredible. You are amazing. I've been looking for you for months and months. I read the article and I told my family, 'Oh my gosh, I could so do this. This is what I want to do, that's who I want to be.'"

I began to feel a little bit like the queen of the world. The article had appeared a whole year ago. She'd remembered and she actually seemed to be interested. For my part, I was finding her really easy to talk to. I began to see the possibilities.

"Let me ask you something," I said. "Would you go up to anyone and say anything to them?"

"Absolutely."

"You wouldn't have any problem with that?"

"No."

She wasn't going to be intimidated. She could pull off what I had in mind.

"How would you like to become a PI?"

I explained that the *Today* show wanted to interview my sister and me, but she couldn't do it.

"I'll do it, sure," she said. "Gosh. Wait a minute. I can't do it because I'm not a private investigator."

"We have two weeks. In two weeks you will be a PI. You'll have stories to tell, you'll have everything."

For the next fourteen days, Mollie was glued to my side. I took her everywhere. As we talked more, we found we had even more in common. We had kids the same age. Mollie and her husband Bill had four children: twenty-year-old Kristina, eighteen-year-old Kellin, sixteen-year-old Staci and ten-year-old Maddie. Bill had taken a post as head of the illustration department of a local university. Mollie and Bill's was a successful union based on spiritual principles, just like mine and Jay's.

Our educational backgrounds dovetailed. I had my degree in social work. As a social worker, I'd concentrated on children's issues. Mollie had a degree in early childhood education and had been a teacher. She could not, she felt, pick up where she had left off teaching, because her body was too impaired, but she needed to earn some money. The part-time, work-from-home PI gig was attractive.

During the two weeks of her intensive PI training, Mollie worked cases with me and I showed her everything I could think of that would help. We ran license plates at the DMV. We searched databanks for criminal histories. She came to court when I had to testify for a custody case. She watched me do intake of a prospective client. We followed people on surveillance.

We did one tricky car surveillance, with me weaving in and out of traffic to keep up. Mollie was unfazed. While I hit the gas and the brake, she fielded cell phone calls from Maddie, and, in the calmest of mom voices, discussed plans for a slumber party that night.

Despite a lot of hard work on both our parts, Mollie did not feel completely confident by the time we were to do the interview. She was afraid that if anyone on the show asked her a question about the technical side of sleuthing, she wouldn't be able to answer. I told her that if it came to that, we'd both be in trouble because Hanady Investigations was low-tech. That was partly to reassure Mollie, but it was also true that I gravitated to the least-complicated, least-expensive option that would get the job done.

Instead of hooking up fancy equipment that could record both sides of a phone conversation and intercept all extensions, I would place a simple tape recorder in a subject's room. It's legal, because Idaho doesn't require me to inform persons they are being taped. We did spring for good GPS trackers. While all GPS devices work on the same principle—picking up radio beams from several satellites orbiting the earth, and using the minute differences in the time it takes the beam to reach the receiver to calculate position—top-of-the-line GPS trackers also show not just where the car is, but how fast it's going and where it stops. You can follow a car in real time on your computer and the information comes with a nice little chart and map. Jan and I had been using a less expensive model that had to be removed from the car and the data downloaded to a computer before you could learn where a vehicle had been. We could do truth testing with an expensive three-hour polygraph—or we could do voice stress analysis with a short phone call, and that was almost always our choice. I was willing to use technology—even embraced some of it—but no matter how cool the device, it would never replace low-tech powers of observation, buffered with mom-smarts and women's intuition.

Despite her qualms, Mollie was truly impressive on the *Today* show. When I viewed the taped interview, I was amazed at how completely capable she was. Meanwhile, MSNBC had invited Hanady to be on *Countdown with Keith Olbermann*, so that meant several more weeks of collaboration.

At the end of the month and a half, I realized that the time Mollie and I had spent together had accomplished more than making her into a fast-track PI. It had turned her into my new partner. We dubbed the reconfigured business Spymoms, reserving Hanady Investigations, as Jan and I had, for formal occasions.

Our workdays fell into a pattern. I called her in the morning and asked, "How do you feel?"

She would say, "Fine," and I would say, "No. How do you *really* feel?"

She would give me the rundown and that would be the last I heard about it for that day. My phone call might get her out of bed, but she was one to suck it up and go on.

Over the years, doctors had misdiagnosed her with everything from lupus to fibromyalgia. Two years before we met, Mollie had finally received the correct diagnosis. Unfortunately, by then the unchecked disease had fused her spine and lumbar region.

Before I met her, Mollie had become mired in her illness and depressed from a combination of accumulating medical bills, chronic pain and diminished mobility. With psoriatic spondylitis, everything hurts, from head to toe. Just swinging her legs to the floor was excruciatingly painful for Mollie, even before she shifted any weight to her feet. She described trying to get her body to do anything as the equivalent of walking through sludge. She wanted, she said, to unzip her body and be pain-free for a minute to see what it felt like.

I had never heard of psoriatic spondylitis until I met Mollie, and I was not alone in this. There was little public awareness of the illness. Because Mollie had a little-known disease with effects that didn't show, people were not especially sympathetic.

Mollie herself lived in a zone beyond empathy. I learned this when I woke with a horrible headache one day. I was just considering whether to stay in bed or what when the phone rang. It was Mollie.

She said, "You're sick, right? You've got a really, really bad headache."

"Right," I said, between clenched teeth, in too much pain to wonder how she knew.

"Okay. I'm going to get a bad headache and yours is going to go away."

Within fifteen minutes my migraine was gone.

Things like that happened a few times. I'm a grounded person. I'm not inclined to put a lot of stock in seemingly inexplicable phenomena. But even I had to acknowledge that Mollie was tuned into a frequency that I just didn't get. It was a little freaky for me when she just *knew* things. I couldn't keep from trying to understand it logically. I'd have to shrug it off and let it go, until the next time.

We had other differences. For Mollie, PI work was about putting together the pieces of a puzzle, while I was into gathering all the pieces together and sifting through it. I'm not an observer of people. I'm the kind of person who wouldn't notice if the guy had on a wedding ring. Mollie, on the other hand, is an extreme observer of people.

Having an intuitive empath on board would prove to be quite useful, I quickly realized.

I got a first look at how handy it could be when we were hired by an out-of-state client to investigate her son's visits with her ex. It was very difficult putting little five-year-old Billy on the plane to Boise to see Daddy, she said, without a clear idea of what went on during those weeklong visits.

While we didn't think we'd find a good excuse to get into the house and film, we knew we could follow them around to see where Dad took the child. It would be helpful for Mom to know if he took his son to the zoo or the local bar, the bookstore or the strip joint. We could do surveillance and see what kind of people came to the house.

The neighborhood was good for surveillance—there was a church parking lot near the house, where we could stay for hours and unobtrusively keep track of who came and went. We camped there and tailed them whenever they left the house.

For a week, Dad and his girlfriend entertained little Billy in some pretty wholesome ways. We tailed them as they visited play parks. We followed them through McDonald's drive-through window. They got him a Happy Meal, and I had fries. They went to Hollywood Video and rented *Lion King* and *Lady and the Tramp*.

The fifth day we were doing surveillance in front of the house, a nice-looking car pulled up and a well-dressed man in his fifties went into the house.

I was hot to call Mom and give her the scoop.

"Reach in back and grab my phone," I said to Mollie, who was in the passenger seat. She began rummaging through my purse.

"I don't see it," she said. "What the hay—"

"Give it here," I said. The front door opened. I could see the man conversing with Dad. She upended the purse and dumped it in the space between the seats. Tissues, lipstick, change, photos, post-its, ibuprofen, lint—no phone.

"Use mine, use mine."

I got Mom on the phone just as the man let the screen door slam behind him. I described him, and she said, "Oh, that's my son's father's dad. Billy's grandfather. He often comes to see Billy."

"What do you want us to do?" I asked her. I believe in checking in with the client a lot.

"Keep on them," she told us. "Just keep watching."

I handed Mollie back her phone.

"I don't believe it," Mollie said to me. "This guy isn't acting very grandfatherly. He stayed away through most of the week. If he's visiting his grandson, that doesn't make sense. Let's call her back."

Again, Mom confirmed that this was the grandfather. We described him in detail, and she was adamant. But Mollie was just as insistent.

"That is *not* the grandfather," she said. "That man is not the grandfather. I'll call him metrosexual at best."

She kept it up and she kept it up until I snapped. "She told us he's the grandpa," I yelled. "Say he's not one more time and I'm going to slap you."

And just to show her once and for all, I got the grandpa's home phone number from Mom and called while "Grandpa" was at her ex's house. To my great surprise, the real grandfather answered the phone.

That left us with a dilemma. If we had the grandfather on the phone, then who was the other guy?

Little Billy left to go back home three days later. He hadn't been harmed. We were done with the case, formally, but I was curious enough to give it one more night to solve the riddle.

I was sitting there patiently with the binoculars trained on the one uncurtained window.

"I'm going for the trash," Mollie said and slipped out of the car. She retrieved the trash and put the big plastic bag in the trunk of my car.

"Thanks," I said. "It was smelling too clean in here. I was just thinking it needed a little spritz of *l'essence de garbage*."

Mollie tapped me on the shoulder, and since I was peering through the binocs, that got me lost. I looked to retrain them on the right spot.

"You don't need them. Look!"

Our mystery guest and Dad were in a clinch.

So darned if Mollie wasn't right. The girl was just a *friend* friend.

"Grandpa" was the father's boyfriend and he was basically living at the house. He had just been making himself scarce while Billy was around. I think it was then that I realized Mollie's intuition, or whatever you want to call it, was a useful tool.

The next day, I went by Mollie's house just in time to see her break into the stash of trash. It wasn't strictly necessary, because we'd already solved the case, but Mollie loved her trash. She dumped it out on a table in her garage.

Big score.

The bag was full of shoes. There were seven pairs of women's shoes in very large sizes—expensive designer shoes with the tags still on. Mollie's and my feet are small, but that didn't stop us trying them on. We looked like kids tripping around in Mom's shoes.

Mollie gave them to her older daughters, whose feet are large enough to wear them.

Trash is a great way to get at the truth. We dig through trash the way an archaeologist sifts through a site. We're both looking for artifacts from which to reconstruct a story. Only for us, the story usually features a deadbeat dad instead of a dead civilization.

One particular father was stiffing his ex—our client—for child support. It was a case of blood from a stone, he told her. Tough times; she had to understand. He was a month behind on the condominium's maintenance fee. He was pretty sure he was going to be laid off.

We staked out the dumpster behind his condo.

We knew there was absolutely no point in pawing through the garbage from thirty-five units. If we were observant, we'd soon figure out his personal "trash footprint."

One person might knot those green garbage bags right down where the trash is. Another person might tie a bow in the pull tie. Still another garbage style might be to leave the bag open or to pack it in paper.

There are as many styles as there are subjects. I could write a trash treatise.

Our man was a shredder. People who shred documents make life more difficult. And his shredder was a cross-cut machine that shreds in two directions—little bitty squares commonly deemed impossible to reconstruct. I figured that was that.

When we got back to my house, Mollie dumped all the pieces into a big cardboard box. She separated out the items that were too small for shredding.

"You cannot be about to do what I think you are," I said. "Girl, you are certifiable."

"No, not really," she said, "Look at these."

She rifled through a small handful of credit cards slips, and at least five of them were from Asiago's, a pricey Boise restaurant. The charges were not small.

"If he can do this five days in a row, he's got money," she said. "It's worth it to see."

Actually, Mollie has obsessive compulsive disorder, and for something like this it's an advantage. She reconstructed the documents like someone else would work a jigsaw puzzle.

Since this was a puzzle in a zillion pieces, all with the same shape, it made me crazy just to watch her. I found her a little scary, all that insane concentration.

The document turned out to be a bank statement. Our guy had a savings account worth more than fifty thousand dollars. With our evidence, our client was able to get more child support, and with more child support, she could afford early intervention for her daughter's learning issues. Life was significantly improved for them both.

Mollie said that for her, reassembling the document was like meditation. She swore that it was so absorbing that it actually functioned as a pain reliever. The intense concentration and Zen-like focus she brought to the task put her in a zone beyond pain for that time. In fact, for Mollie, a lot of PI work had that unsought but important benefit. The concentration the job required was a pretty effective pain blocker. I was in heaven. Talk about your balanced partnership. For the time that she was tailing a car, or talking a client down from the emotional ledge, or picking through someone's trash, Mollie was distracted from her pain. It was one heck of a perk.

This was why she was also proving superb at surveillance. I thought so much time alone in a car might be boring or lonely, but Mollie said that for her, as a confirmed carpool mom and driver of Maddie and Maddie's friends, quiet time alone was not necessarily a bad thing.

Since Mollie liked surveillance so much, I generously allowed her to do the lion's share. She made sure that the kids were covered, then she put on comfortable clothes, stocked her vehicle with her binoculars, camera and her stun baton—a device that resembles a folded-up umbrella and delivers four hundred thousand volts. It's not lethal, but it's enough to drop a big man. Then, she liked nothing better than to settle comfortably into her vehicle and wait for her subject to appear. While waiting, she occupied herself with grocery lists. When the subject showed, Mollie went through her routine—a few Hail Mary's and the Lord's Prayer. She would wait for the car to pull out and another car to get in between. Then, her version of moving surveillance was this: You go through red lights and yell at other people to get them to get out of your way.

Her intuition was almost as good as a tracking device. She often got a feeling just before the front door opened and the subject emerged. Once on the road, she often knew just when and where the subject was going to turn.

Pretexting remained my strong point. When we first started working together, Mollie had a hard time getting past the possibility that pretexting was just lying, and she didn't know how she was going to tell her kids not to do something when she was doing it herself. However, it wasn't long before she, like me, saw that it often got us information that could really help people. She came to see it as acting a part for a good cause.

Time after time, the pretext got us information that would have been very difficult and time-consuming to unearth any other way. An early cheater case featured a suspect we had followed for two weeks. We were waiting for her to make a misstep—or, at least, to give us an opening. It took us a long time to find something we had in common. She presented a smooth, impermeable surface. We weren't getting anywhere.

We knew from her husband that her one outside interest was Race for the Cure. I thought, *Well, why not? I'm a cancer survivor.* I called her and said we wanted to be volunteers for Race for the Cure and we would take her to lunch to find out about it. By the time we got to dessert, we'd heard all about the hottest affair of her life. She just told us everything. Everything. We used Taking the Mistress to Lunch for many other cases after that.

Occasionally pretexting did backfire. I had used a pretext to try to find out the location of a particular subject, a nineteen-year-old, who was already a deadbeat dad. He had walked away from his apartment, but he was supposed to be still couch-surfing around Boise. We knew he was friendly with one young lady who was a minor.

I called her family and said that we were concerned because we knew their young daughter was friends with this man, and it was suspected that this man, who was a dubious character, had planned to leave town. Their daughter might have left town with him. Were they aware of her current whereabouts? I thought they would let on if he was staying with them.

As I clicked my phone shut, it rang almost immediately. It was from someone who had located our subject. I decided to call back and let that family off the hook. I got in touch with the dad and told him, "Look, that was a ruse to try to find out where this man is living. We don't think your daughter's in any particular danger. No one's trying to do her any harm."

"Who do you think you are," he screamed, "to call me up and lie about my child? Who gave you that right?" He was incredibly angry. I had thought he would be relieved to know she was okay, but it turned out I still had a lot to learn about people.

Chapter 8
The Stupid Pretext

ONE NIGHT, WE FOUND OURSELVES IN A NEIGHBORHOOD that was more than a little ragged.

It was a stone-dark block of three houses in an industrial part of town. We were parked there to hand papers to Amber, a woman who was going to serve time for driving under the influence. The front yard was dirt, the backyard, desert. It had a lonely feel. A pickup truck with a bunch of guys had pulled up behind us, blocking us in. I felt a prickle of fear. If we encountered trouble, we weren't likely to find help.

Our subject's ex, who wanted custody of the children, had hired an attorney, and the attorney had hired us. We were to serve the summons, see what we could glean about her lifestyle, and keep an eye on her. She was used to just taking off when she was served papers, we were told. She probably intended to leave with the kids. She had a drug-dealing boyfriend who lived out-of-state.

While we waited, Mollie considered how to approach this tricky situation.

"Let's do Lost Dog," she said. "Or how about Estate Sale?"

"*Estate* Sale? Look around you."

This was clearly the land of the garage sale, if it was anything at all. And it was winter. Not garage sale season.

We did have choices. Among the various pretexts I used to knock on a subject's door were Lost Dog, New to the Neighborhood, Looking to Buy Property and We're Lost—always good because we could say it was hard to read the map by the dim porch light and get an invite inside.

"Well, so, if you don't like Estate Sale, let's pick one," she said. "Let's make a plan."

"No, let's just go for it." I was learning that Mollie liked to overthink the pretext. When she hesitated and began to speak in that slow, deliberate way, I wanted to throttle her. But I found that if I just charged ahead, she followed and she always caught on.

"How about this," Mollie said. "Let's tell her we're from some group that helps women who have to serve time. We could call it Women's Alliance for Children and Mothers. Or, what would we call it?"

"We'd call it *stupid*," I said. "That's a stupid idea, Mollie. No one in her right mind would believe that."

The truth was, we were both a little testy.

I'd driven, and Mollie hated it when I drove. I'm fast, I have to admit. She'd made me pay for that by driving me nuts. The whole time, on the way here, she told me which way to go. All I wanted to know was if I could get over, and she said yes without really having a clue. She just stuck her hand out the window and motioned the cars to slow down because we were coming, ready or not.

So after the lovely trip to the subject's house, I parked halfway down the small block. It was cold, it was tedious, and we had been there for more than an hour. I wanted to climb into my own comfortable bed and watch *Survivor* or reruns of *Unsolved Mysteries* with a Diet Coke in one hand and a Tootsie Pop peppermint sucker in the other.

Jay complains he's had to remove more than one sucker from my drooling mouth and soda can from my hand after I've drifted off to sleep sitting up in bed, but I'll believe it when I see it. Of course, since I'm asleep at the time, I can never see it.

The sound of a misfiring car engine intruded on my reverie. Our subject pulled into the driveway, cut the engine and killed the headlights. She emerged with arms loaded and multiple grocery bags hanging off her wrists. She kicked the car door closed behind her.

The kids got out and ran into the house.

We didn't want her to go in and lock the door. We caught her on the front step with her key already in the lock. It had to be quick, whatever we did.

"Excuse me," I said, keeping my voice even and unthreatening. "Can we speak to you for just a minute? Are you Amber Riley?

She said that yes, she was.

I handed her the paperwork.

She took one look and crumpled against the doorframe. She went into some kind of shock. I said, "But. We're from the group Women's Alliance for Children and Mothers. We offer help to women who have to serve time. Youch!"

Mollie, behind me, had my upper arm in a pincers grip. I'd just used the ploy I'd given her such grief over. I had called it stupid and then I had used it. I turned and saw that her eyebrows had disappeared into her bangs. She shook her head in disgust.

We didn't get past the front step with Amber, who was understandably eager to close the door on us. However, she nodded a grudging yes when we asked if we could come back to visit with her and bring her a gift basket.

Once we got back in the car, we high-fived, and then when we tried to call the attorney, we both started laughing so hard that we had to call back to leave the message on his machine. He must have thought we were truly insane.

Mollie's pretext was actually a really good one, in the end. It gave us a reason to go back and visit Amber again and again. We did help her, in a way. We went to Penney's and bought the kids toys and clothes. We got her gift certificates to Wal-Mart. We got a basket and fixed it up nice for her, with bath oil and makeup and some good shampoo and such. We got her to talk to us. She told us that she planned on moving. If we talked to her in a couple of days, she'd know just where. She said, "I don't understand it; he seems to know my every move. He must have a private investigator watching me."

I might have felt a twinge of guilt if I didn't know that this woman's plan was to hide young kids from their natural father and hand them off to her felon boyfriend. The biological dad was our client and we both liked him a lot. I empathized with our client and not so much with the woman whose behavior had created painful situations for her children.

Eventually, Amber did wind up going to jail. Dad got custody.

Mollie didn't let me forget the Stupid Pretext for a long time after that case. Whenever we'd brainstorm about what tack to take with a new situation, she'd say, "Well, I have an idea.... But, then again, it's probably just, you know, another ineffectual, pointless Stupid Pretext."

Our pretexting teamwork did get smoother, over time. We developed quite a nice repertoire. Garage Sale remained one of our favorites. We came to the door with a clipboard and a bunch of papers all typed up. We talked about a garage sale we were planning. It would be a neighborhood garage sale. We asked if they wanted to participate. We would do all the advertising. We would have day care for the kids and provide coffee and doughnuts for everyone who participated.

Mollie thought it sounded so great, we should really put on a garage sale like this sometime.

Mollie and I were learning to work together. We were truly becoming partners. At the same time we were bonding, we were instinctively enlarging the circle to include people from our lives. We were the opposite of the hard-boiled detective, the *film noir* dude who cinches his trench coat and disappears into the night alone. We were Spymoms, and we made PI work a family affair. Sooner or later, everyone got into the act.

Jay helped out with surveillance of a deadbeat dad. We'd been doing the surveillance day after day and we needed a break, so we sent Jay to the subdivision. We'd sat unobtrusively in the car while waiting for something to happen. Jay's method was different. He brought along a lawn chair and sat there out in the open, smoking a big cigar.

Kids playing basketball asked him, "What are you doing here?"

"I'm doing surveillance on a deadbeat dad down the street," he replied, blowing out a mouthful of smoke. "Mind if I sit here?"

They let him use the bathroom. They even brought him a glass of lemonade.

Once, I called on Jay for help when I was supposed to tail the subject in a cheater case. Mollie was busy elsewhere, and I thought the guy could be headed way out of town, so I wanted the company.

Jay jumped at the invitation. Jay never believed me when I complained about how hard it was not to lose someone and, at the same time, not be noticed. He thought it couldn't possibly be as hard as I made it sound. This would be a chance to prove his point.

We waited outside the subject's apartment for a few hours. When he finally emerged and got into his Gran Torino, Jay waited for thee cars to pass and then pulled out into the traffic.

Jay did everything just right. He was feeling pretty savvy and on top of things. We followed the guy out of town, and were headed to the country on a two-lane road. We came to a four-way stop, still three cars behind. While we advanced to the stop sign, Jay took the opportunity to turn to me and say, "You see. It isn't as hard as you make it out to be. You just have to—"

Just as he said that, a farmer pulling a big load of sprinkler pipe turned onto the road ahead of us. And proceeded at twenty miles per hour. Jay couldn't pass because of the oncoming traffic. Our subject was long gone and Jay had to eat crow.

We also turned to friends. Nurse Maggie was pulled into the PI world when she gave us permission to park in front of her house because a subject we were watching lived on her street. She almost blew our cover, though, because she kept walking over to the car to chat and hang out.

We were occasionally joined on surveillance by people who were interested in becoming PIs. A Web site called VocationVacations would pair us up with people seeking a change of career or just looking for the fun of exploring a new field. The twelve people we mentored between 2004 and 2007 each spent two days job-shadowing us while we kept an eye on them. At the end of their two-day VocationVacation, they usually had a better idea of what PI work was about. Even if they didn't decide to become full-time private investigators, they had fun with us.

Most of them.

We had a Vocationer along when we had to serve a summons in a dicey Southside Nampa neighborhood. Nampa, which has a crime rate to rival downtown Denver, is a focus for gang activity in southwest Idaho. As we rolled down the street where our subject lived—a street lined with potholes and junker trucks—a dog streaked right in front of my car. I slammed on the brakes. It looked like a mean dog, and it was the kind of neighborhood where the dog-of-choice would be a pit bull. Mollie braced herself against the dashboard. I felt a jolt as the Vocationer, who wasn't buckled up, rebounded off the back of my seat.

I love dogs, but I don't trust a rottie or a pit. Jay once had a showdown with a rotweiller in our Denver neighborhood. He faced the monster dog alone, sort of like Atticus Finch in *To Kill a Mockingbird*, except that Atticus had a rifle and Jay had a plastic toy shovel I'd tossed out the front door when he called for a weapon. He actually faced down the dog by standing his ground. I admired him, but I wasn't going there.

I caught Vocationer's eye in the rearview mirror. She was clearly thinking something along the lines of, "What are we doing here?" I could have told her what Mollie always says, which is that we lack the fear chip. Fear just doesn't enter our heads much.

We all went to the door of the house where the woman we were supposed to be serving lived. There was an old tabby cat sleeping on a sun-bleached picnic table in the front yard. There was a manila envelope tacked on the door. It had a penciled message that read: "Go away. I'm not here." We knocked on the door anyway, but no one answered. We headed back to the car, and I was almost to the corner when the mail truck turned in and began its halting progress down the street.

"Stop," Mollie said suddenly. "We're not leaving. She'll come out and get the mail."

"What are you talking about?" I put the car in gear and started to drive down the street.

"People like this always get their mail. They think there might be money in the mail."

I shook my head, but I turned around in a driveway and we idled there at the end of the long block.

No sooner had the mail truck departed than the door we'd been watching opened, and a heavyset woman in pink sweats and slippers padded down the walk.

"Hurry!" Mollie said. "Pink is on the move, pink is on the move!"

I hit the gas like you cannot believe. Mollie swayed, clinging with both hands to the ceiling strap. I slowed next to our subject and rolled down my window. "Somebody hit your car, somebody hit your car."

The Vocationer caught the drift and rolled down her window too. "Yes, they did. I saw them."

The woman said, "What, what?" and bent to pick up the mail she was fumbling. She wasn't taking in what we'd told her.

I said, "Somebody hit your car. On a bike. And dented your car."

"Oh my gosh." That cleared the cobwebs. She loped down the side-walk, toward a red Camry. We rolled along beside her.

I said to Mollie, "Do it. Do it *now*."

"Is your name Jody Black?"

"Yes, it is." She was so off-balance that she responded without thinking about it.

"Well, here are your papers," Mollie said, shoving them out the window at her. "Oh, and we were just kidding. Nobody hit your car."

We drove off, laughing like maniacs.

Jay helped us from time to time, and Vocationers were fun when we had them, but our most enthusiastic junior partner was Maddie, Mollie's youngest. My own kids were older and off doing their own thing by this point. Scott enjoyed hearing about cases, but was more stoked about having the house to himself when PI work took me out of town while Jay was gone. Jeff wasn't thrilled about sleuthing because he thought it was dangerous, although I could call on him to discuss the ethical dilemmas sleuthing raised. Christine had graduated and was seriously dating a man named Ben, whom she would eventually marry.

The older kids, when they were around, took our sleuthing for granted. Being a PI was just the norm to them, just something Mom did. Mom drove the carpool, Mom picked apart people's trash.

On an old VCR tape, between the segments where everyone is opening Christmas presents and the ones that feature kids blowing out birthday candles, is a moment when Mollie's daughter, Kristina, approaches Mollie and me as we sort through trash on a worktable in the garage, looking for evidence.

She pauses to ask, "Hey. What are you guys doing?"

We say, "Oh, we're going through someone's garbage."

"Huh. Typical."

She rolls her eyes, shrugs, saunters off.

Maddie and her friends were willing to look through trash, although garbage was losing its appeal as the teen years advanced. Still, Maddie glamorized us, telling her buddies, "My mom's a spy."

Maddie adored sleuthing and her friends did too. Our deal with them was that their parents had to give permission for extra kids to come along. They had to be good and they couldn't get out of the car unless specifically invited. There were places we would take them and places we would not, and that's how it was. It was understood that if they wanted to be with us on the job, they had to observe PI protocol and pee outside, even if they thought it was gross. Even with those rules, Maddie and her friends were often happy to join us on surveillance and do their home-work in the backseat.

Sometimes they played a more active role. Once, Mollie was working a guy cheater case for a wife, and we had agreed that placing a tracker on his car made sense, because we'd be able to see when he was at the mistress's house. We put the tracker on his lower left bumper while he was visiting his lady friend and decided it would stay in place for two days.

The problem was, we then needed some way to get the tracker back. He lived in a cul-de-sac and kept his car in his garage. Even with the garage door open, it would be tricky to get the tracker off because he was the sort of guy to be out in his yard, puttering under the hood. And even if he wasn't out in the yard, the cul-de-sac meant that our every move would be observed by a whole circle of neighbors. These people were really into Neighborhood Watch too. So we had to figure out an ironclad ploy.

We needed help. Time to call in the preteen investigators.

Maddie was at a friend's house nearby, so the girls skateboarded on over. They circled the cul-de-sac to create a diversion. They had brought a ball, and Mollie thought it might be good if they rolled the ball up onto the subject's lawn a few times, so that anyone watching would get used to seeing them go onto his property. Eventually, they could "accidentally" send the ball into the garage. Mollie would then have an excuse to go in and grab the tracker.

So they did it, in a subtle way. They threw that ball around enough so that anyone watching would be lulled into believing they were just clumsy kids. Then, they rolled it into the garage and went over to a neighbor who was trimming a hedge and made enough noise to distract the man's attention while Mollie did her best to run into the garage. She couldn't really sprint because her disease doesn't allow it. She did manage to half-run, half-limp up his drive and get hold of the tracker.

The tracker gave us information about when he was likely to be at his mistress's house. That saved a lot of time, because we could do a drive-by instead of sitting and waiting in front of the house for hours. On one such pass by the house, Mollie saw his car in her driveway.

She needed proof, but she had left her camera in her other car. She ran to the local market to buy a disposable camera. Just inside the front door, there was a display of fruit roll-ups on sale, and the price was really good, so how could she pass that up? Then she remembered she was out of milk, so she nabbed a couple cartons and, while she was running past the cold cereals, picked one out, because she had promised the kids that they could try a new kind, and here was one that looked like it might appeal to them and it only had eight grams of sugar.

She got back to the site in time to catch a really sterling shot of our cheater dude leaning out of his car window for that last, lingering kiss. Mollie didn't forget to shoot the license plates while she was at it. She got the film developed at a one-hour photo shop and dropped the pictures off to our client's attorney. That money shot made the case.

The younger kids did so well helping us that Mollie founded a Junior Investigator's Club. The club would, she felt, give young women a place to feel competent and daring. They could be members only if they didn't experiment with sex, drugs or alcohol. Being in the club made them feel special.

One time, Maddie and I joined forces to play a trick on Mollie. Anything to liven up a long surveillance.

We were after a well-known society man in Boise. His wife thought he was using prostitutes, but we had to catch him at it. We were parked outside an apartment building that he owned. If he left, we'd be positioned to follow.

Mollie had to use the facilities, but of course there were no facilities to speak of. If she went off looking for a bathroom, we might lose him. But Mollie was desperate, so she walked across the street to where she could see a bush up against a fence. While she was crouching behind the bush, I sent Maddie across the street and told her to act as if she were some stranger walking by, just to give Mollie a little adrenaline rush.

Mollie's malady kicked in—her hips locked and she couldn't get up. There she was, in a most inelegant position, about, she thought, to find herself eye to ankle with a stranger.

At the last moment she managed to haul herself, hand over hand, up the fence. Luckily, she had the grace to find it funny.

Mollie and I had bonded and we'd meshed work life with family and friends. We joked that we shared one brain because our strengths were so balanced. She was teaching me to be more observant and I was teaching her to think on her feet. In the process, we'd also become more skilled at investigation of all sorts. I really saw it when we were invited to investigate a radio talk show host.

By this time, Mollie and I were featured on the radio regularly. We appeared once a month on a local station. It was not a giant deal, but it was fun. They'd have people call in and we'd answer their questions—just silly stuff.

As word of our business spread, we sometimes did radio interviews for radio stations in other cities.

One time, when we were invited to be guests on a talk show out of Pocatello, our radio host, Barry, surprised us with a challenge to investigate him and return the next week with the results.

"I'm thinking you won't find much," he said on the air. "You've heard of the life that's an open book? Well, this book is so closed it's not even on the shelf." He was pumping up the drama for the benefit of listeners, but underneath that, I felt his skepticism. I had the impression that he liked us, but he didn't see us as particularly skilled.

As soon as the show was over, we made a beeline for his BMW in the parking lot. I copied down the plate.

"What are you doing right now?" I asked Mollie.

"Staci has to see the orthodontist, but not until four, so I have about an hour to spare."

"Let's do it. Head for Boise and I'll meet you at the DMV at three. You've got the forms, because I looked for them this morning and I couldn't find them." The Idaho Motor Vehicle Record Request form and the Driver's License Record form were the ones we needed, and we kept a stack on hand. As licensed PIs we had access and they would tell us a lot—date of birth, social security number and home address, for openers.

"I don't know where they are in the car, but they're in there some-where." Mollie nodded.

We headed straight to the DMV. It might have been more efficient to have called in the request for information, but we would have missed the personal contact with the DMV people. Our favorite clerk, Dale, was working a window.

"You look skinnier every time I see you," I told him. It was true. He had a thin face made longer by a brush cut. "Mollie's got the forms."

"We're going to bring you some doughnuts," Mollie said. She was fill-ing out the forms from notes she'd made on the back of a used-up block of checks. "Or is it *take*? 'Take you some doughnuts?' No, it's *bring*."

"You're doing it again," I said.

"What is she doing?" Dale wanted to know.

"She's being the language police. She keeps track of language."

Mollie turned the page over to fill in the back of the form. "Sometimes I don't catch it in time. It'll be two days later."

"This from someone who pronounces Oregon as Oregone."

"That's like tomato, to*mah*to."

"No it's not. You look it up in the dictionary. Look at the pronuncia-tion," I said.

Mollie stopped writing and peered at her notes. "This is ridiculous. I can't read my own writing. Does that look like an *L*?"

"So how's Spy Bear?" I asked Dale, to change the subject. I put out my hand and Dale placed a tiny stuffed bear on my palm.

"He's not happy," Dale said. "He says you don't visit enough." Spy Bear had been in my Christmas basket for Dale.

"Here." Mollie passed him the completed forms.

"Are we doing registrations on this?"

"We want the vehicle record and we want his driving record," I said. "The full meal deal."

Dale ticked away on his keyboard. "They say there's never been any plate like that."

"Did we mess up?" I narrowed my eyes at the form. "Did we miss a number?"

"No," Mollie said, "I was really careful, writing it down. That's why I can't figure it out."

Dale ticked away again for a minute.

"The format is right," he said, studying his screen.

"But it still doesn't come up," Mollie said. "Classic."

"No, wait. Here it is," Dale said. "He has three different ones. I see motorcycle, car, truck."

"I want them all," Mollie said. "Lay it on me"

"Do you want historical or do you want current?"

"Give us everything you've got," I said. Dale disappeared to pull the documents off the printer. He returned with a stack. Our host had himself quite a driving record of suspensions, DUIs, and fender benders. The list pointed to a problem with alcohol.

I wrote a check for the DMV fees and handed it to Dale.

"You tell Spy Bear we'll see him soon," I said. "You too."

"I'm always here." He smiled, ruefully. "It's not fishing season, so I'm not taking any days off."

Next, we checked Barry out for a criminal record on the Idaho courts Web site, which has both criminal and civil records for Idaho. We didn't think we'd really find anything. We were simply demonstrating what was possible.

We thought it would be a hoot to get hold of his high school yearbook.

We knew he had grown up in Boise, so we only had four public high schools and a handful of private schools to contact. We went to the schools, and I did a pretext, telling the people in the office that I had graduated from the school, but that I'd lost my high school yearbook. Would it be all right if I looked through their archives? I found the book from Barry's graduating year at one of the schools. There he was, hair all poufed out and sideburns to his jawline.

The caption by his photograph listed clubs he'd been part of and which sports he'd done. The prom picture was a major coup, because it listed his date's name.

Then I had an idea. I looked in the yearbooks bracketing his year. I went ten years before and ten after. I found all his siblings. I would be able to trace them and get a wealth of personal information.

Next we looked online. When I first began investigating, finding information online was confusing. The problem wasn't that there was too little information out there, but too much. I was always weeding through what seemed like thousands of sites.

I was more likely, in the beginning, to go for sites that offered one kind of information. For instance, I could find out the name of a subject's bank by going to the Federal Reserve Web site and plugging in the routing number found on the bottom of checks. To find bankruptcy records, I could use PACER, a service of the Administrative Office of United States Courts that gives access to court documents.

Now, instead of always searching through many different databases, I started with a public record retrieval company that bundled different searches onto one site tailored to the needs of law enforcement, bail bondsmen, attorneys, insurance companies and other "need to know" professionals.

I could search people by name and last known state, by social security number. Or I could find them by looking up spouses and relatives.

I still used individual sites sometimes, but this way I didn't feel like I was stumbling around blindfolded. The process of searching through so many sites had one fun aspect, however. I'd stumbled onto some truly bizarre and quirky databases. There are sites that can locate a dead celebrity's grave or read a transcript of the black-box recording before a plane crash. You can get the addresses of every known meth lab in the US, or find the names of doctors who've defaulted on their student loans. You can even poke around in a national database of shoplifters and crooked retail employees.

The next week, we went back to Barry with a folder at least an inch thick, just crammed with his personal information. We had a list of all the women he had dated. We had the names of all his family members and his previous wives and quite a lot about his drinking problem. All the radio stations he had worked at. We interviewed people to see why he'd left his jobs and we knew if each had been voluntary, and if not, why he'd been let go.

We did have a few scruples. We didn't detail his bankruptcies on air. We didn't read anything that he hadn't already seen first.

There was one exception. In the course of our investigations, we had found out that his favorite niece was pregnant. No one in the family knew it yet, but I got her permission to announce it on the show.

I said, on the air, "I know something even you don't know about your family. I know that your niece is pregnant."

That one blew him away. He didn't doubt us after that.

Chapter 9

Grandma and Monique

AFTER THAT RADIO SHOW, WE GOT A CALL FROM A woman whose friend had heard us on the air. At the time, we had no idea that this would become a seemingly endless case and one of the toughest that we would ever face. We agreed to meet the prospective client at our "office," a downtown Denny's. The restaurant is located about halfway between Mollie's house and my own.

Mollie and I got there a half hour before the new client. This was by design. Before coffee, before we ordered food, we bowed our heads and said a prayer together. This is how we'd come to open a new case. We asked for protection for ourselves. We asked that we be able to do something of value for these people, and, if nothing else, that we not cause harm to them. Asking for guidance was important because we knew we weren't omniscient. We don't necessarily know what's best in a given situation.

A woman we would come to think of as Grandma walked up to the table.

"Are you Valerie?" she asked.

When I nodded, she wedged herself into the seat across from us. Without consulting each other, both Mollie and I inched the table closer to us. Grandma was in her late sixties, a big gal in a lavender pantsuit. Her grizzled hair had seen too many permanents and her raw hands too much work. She looked at my own extended hand blankly before clasping it for a millisecond. She refolded her arms across her ample chest, fingers tucked into armpits. She looked like someone who'd rather eat glass than confide family secrets to strangers.

Mollie started with small talk and gently led Grandma to her story. Mollie was a natural listener. She listened with sympathy and empathy to a story, and heard everything a prospective client needed to say.

I could see Grandma warm to Mollie, who had already earned the unofficial title of Spymoms Friend-Maker. Grandma still seemed a shade hesitant though.

I was the Taskmaster. I kept things on track. I jumped in to help her focus, "Can you tell us about what made you decide to contact us?" I smiled encouragingly. "And what it is you want us to do for you?" Sometimes clients don't really know.

She met my gaze full-on for the first time. I looked into those hooded eyes and saw shrewdness that couldn't be camouflaged. I saw awareness and determination and something else—an amused glint—as she watched me wake up, with a little jolt, to the realization that I'd been had. I reshuffled my impression of her, kicking myself for having been blinded by her cloak of invisibility.

"You want to know why I'm here? This is why I'm here." She took a stack of photographs from her pocketbook and spread them in an arc, face up, in one smooth gesture. The photos were oriented to Mollie and me. They were pictures of what looked like the same child at different ages.

"May I?" I nabbed a photo of the child at three or four, in a formal studio pose.

"Oh, is the little girl your granddaughter?" Mollie pointed to another photo, a picture of a child smiling up from a sandbox. "What a cutie."

"She is, isn't she?" Instantly animated, Grandma leaned into the conversation. "That's my precious darling Shirleen. She's four in that picture, but she turned six last month. I made that outfit she has on. I gave it to her and she said, 'Grandma. I want to put on the pretty dress right now.' Here she is at one day old. Here she is at three years." She handed Mollie a shot of a winsome child holding up the edges of her dress in an old-fashioned curtsey.

I was looking at another, a photo of the child smiling up into the face of an old man.

"There she is with Grandpa. That was the Christmas before he left us. Stroke."

Mollie and I said "I'm sorry" in unison. Grandma nodded. "Here we are at the Grand Canyon. A Canadian gal took that shot. Nice lady."

Shirleen sat on the shoulders of a beefy man in his thirties. The child held aloft a cowboy hat, presumably his.

"That your son?" I asked.

"Shirleen's dad, my Jimmy," she said. "Not the sharpest tool, but a good heart. Shirleen got my brains. She was reading at four." Grandma sighed. She leaned back in the booth and eyed us speculatively. There was a longish pause. A shadow passed over her face. "Well, I guess you need to meet her mother, then, don't you."

Grandma dug around in her purse and flipped a dog-eared photo onto the table. Mollie turned it face up. I saw a woman, early to mid-thirties, in low-slung jeans and a crop top. She looked back over one shoulder with a sultry pout. The short top revealed an elaborate tattoo across her lower back. The image was of double pistols pointed south.

"That's Monique, my daughter-in-law," Grandma said flatly. "When my son came home and told me he'd met a nice woman in a bar, I said to him, 'You don't meet nice women in bars, Jimmy. You meet trashy women in bars.' I should know. I was a dealer at the casino for how many years?"

Mollie and I exchanged a look. She had spread the photos like a deck of cards.

"Well, he was taken with her. I could see that. They got together and she did the one good thing she ever did, which was to have Shirleen. Not that she had a whole bunch of interest in it. She did not. She already had a son and a daughter and didn't have much time for them, either. Jimmy was the one to change the diapers and all of that. He'd bring the baby to stay with us and I had no problem with that. Not at all. Not Grandpa, neither. He just loved that baby girl.

"She started stepping out on Jimmy. Well. She probably was the whole way through and he just finally caught her. Then she divorced him and she got custody. She's an ex-prostitute. She's doing drugs and the boyfriend's no good. So that's a good idea. Give her custody. She's neglectful and abuseful. I have nightmares about what she's doing to that child."

"That has to be really hard," Mollie said.

"Harder for Shirleen," Grandma said, grim.

"Is there any direct evidence of physical abuse, like bruising and so forth?" I asked. "If there is, did you document it or report it?"

"No I did not," she said. "Jimmy saw it and I didn't, so it's hearsay. We called children's services but nothing happened. Imagine that."

"We could put some kind of tape-recording device with Shirleen," I said. "We put it in a toy, like a teddy bear. We've done that a lot."

"The way you approach it is important," Mollie said. "Don't approach it like, 'You're spying on Mommy.' She would have a sense of fear when she saw her mom if she's spying on her. She might not be able to articulate it, but it would be there."

"Wait a minute. Actually, it's not hearsay if he's going for custody," I said. "That's what we're doing, right? You're looking to help your son get custody."

"No. I want custody myself," she said. "I'm betting that you find enough dirt on her that I get it. You're two sharp gals. Let's double down and take her."

Mollie looked at me. I looked at Mollie.

We knew we didn't have the whole story yet. Why was she making an end run around the child's father? A man who had changed all those diapers. There had to be a piece missing.

"I have to excuse myself a minute," I said. "You both keep on. Don't wait for me." It was a strategy calculated to give Grandma a chance to speak to one person, instead of two. If the material was tough, it might make it easier to confide. I saw Mollie pull out her pink notebook. That notebook is her file. She has her notes for every case in there.

When I returned, Grandma had more photos out and Mollie was looking through them. I had hoped my absence would encourage Grandma to open up, but no.

"Look," I said. "Before we can help you, we need to know what we're dealing with. Is there anything else that we should know that we don't?"

Then it came out. There was a complication. Jimmy had been slapped with a charge of sexual offender for "inappropriately touching" Monique's older daughter, then thirteen—a scene that Monique had brokered, Grandma said. After that, Jimmy had moved back home. He could forget custody and she knew it. He'd have a better chance of getting custody of his daughter if he had murdered someone. The kick in the head was that even though Grandma, not her son, was seeking custody, his living with her could make gaining custody harder. I could tell she'd already thought about it, but had put it away. Denial trumps intelligence any day, when the stakes are this high.

I was scrupulous when it came to fleshing out the PI process for a new client. I explained to Grandma that she would give us a retainer and we would work off of that. We would only do what she wanted. If she wanted ten hours of surveillance, we would do ten. If she wanted six, we would stop at six.

We told Grandma the truth: Monique's physical appearance wasn't going to mean much. She could have twenty tattoos and it wouldn't matter. Women could wear low-cut clothing if they wanted to. They wouldn't lose their kids for that.

It would take definitive evidence of major abuse to get the child back. Every state has different custody laws and every judge has a personal slant on those laws. In other words, there are factors that are variable and beyond our control. It's not easy to wrest custody from a mom and I wanted Grandma to understand this.

Furthermore, I told her, surveillance might not produce the definitive proof of abuse she was after. People generally do not stand framed in the open doorway to light up a bong or beat their kids. They do not take their children onto the front lawn to sexually abuse them. Not that that was necessarily happening, I hastened to add.

Grandma flipped open a checkbook and fixed me with those hooded eyes, pen at the ready.

"How much?"

Mollie dove into this case headfirst, the way she always did. Soon she was spending four hours a day following Monique around. If Grandma called and said, I think they're at such-and-such a place, Mollie jumped in her car and drove over there and did surveillance until way after midnight. She was not very good about billing her time, so she wasn't necessarily getting paid for all that work. The case was destined to be a quick burnout, at that rate.

On top of that, we were getting a lot of business now. Sometimes we needed help with the surveillance end of things. We were collecting a little group of people who were already investigators, but who felt we had something further we could teach them. They worked for us, from time to time, as independent contractors. Sherri Arey was the first contractor to come on board.

We called in Sherri to do some of the surveillance on Monique. Sherri was a gun-toting dynamo in a five-foot two-inch package. She came to Spymoms with a background in elder-abuse investigation and child custody. She was happy, though, to pick up on our way of doing things.

I got support from Sherri because, like me, she is a cancer survivor. We have a bond. We've had an experience that "civilians" haven't.

She followed Monique to McCall, a town close to ski resort Tamarack, where a Mardi Gras festival was under way. We knew Monique was headed that way, because she'd told her ex. Sherri had a relatively easy time following her, because Monique was driving a Honda in a bright shade of blue, with a little fin on the back and a plate that read MOOVTYU.

At Tamarack, Sherri donned the mask and beads she had brought and tracked Monique and friends on foot through the town, where the festival was happening. Sherri followed them into a bar, where she got an inspiration.

She went up to the group where they were hanging out at the bar—Monique, her thug boyfriend and their drug-dealing buddies.

"Hey," she said to Monique's boyfriend, "Can I get a picture with you? I want to make my ex jealous." She handed one of them her camera.

"Sure, baby," boyfriend said and—pulling Monique to his other side—draped his big self over Sherri, who is tiny. As the camera was snapping away, his hand came slithering down and grabbed her breast. She was being groped through her blue angora sweater.

Occupational hazard for the unwary pretexter.

Sherri checked in with us later.

"They invited me up to their suite to party," she said, "but, you know, I thought maybe not."

We definitely understood that, we told her. Partying with drug-dealers was not part of her job description.

Three days after the ski getaway, Sherri and Mollie were following Monique's car. Mollie thought she could see Monique and the boyfriend drinking in the front seat. They were all over the road, so that looked promising. It was also incredibly disturbing, because Mollie was pretty sure the little girl was in the backseat.

Sherri was in good with the cops, so she called them and said, "I'm following someone who's driving drunk. Can you check her out?"

A couple of minutes later, she had heard sirens, and Monique was pulled over and given the breathalyzer test. One DUI wouldn't impede parental rights, but it was a start.

Mollie and Sherri had to testify in court. I went along for the ride and to coach Mollie, who hadn't given a lot of testimony. It was an important feature of our job. We often had to go to court when cases we gathered evidence for came before a judge.

Mollie wore a black linen sheath with white piping and a white Panama fedora with black grosgrain ribbon. It was a very stylish outfit.

"I'm having a bad hair day," she hissed at me.

"You look fabulous," I said, and meant it.

Neither of us knew that courtroom etiquette forbids the wearing of hats.

On the list of courtroom no-no's, hats are right up there with chewing gum and dark glasses.

The case was straightforward. Mollie's recollections were concise. Monique lost her license for a while. She was court-ordered to attend AA.

Everyone else had left the courtroom and I was still gathering up my paperwork when the judge motioned for Mollie to approach the bench.

"Don't you ever come into this courtroom with a hat and disrespect this court again," she said.

"Are you kidding me?" Mollie said.

"No." The judge shook her head. "That's so disrespectful."

Mollie turned to go, but she just had to deliver the parting shot.

"Lady, you need to take a nap."

I waited until we were clear of the courthouse steps before I confronted her.

"Mollie. Don't you realize she could have thrown you in jail for saying that?"

Mollie was unperturbed. "She was so crabby." She shrugged. "She really did need a nap."

The relative ease with which we'd nailed Monique with the DUI led me to conclude we could give Grandma's attorney enough ammo to press her case within, say, six months.

Mollie already cared about that little girl. She jumped into her car, day or night, and sat outside Monique's house hour after hour, praying for someone to make the misstep that would deliver the child and end her nightmare, as well as the Grandma's anguish. With a little luck and a lot of Mollie's focus, I was convinced that we'd soon nail Monique with a few more DUIs.

Now, when I think about how optimistic I was over that DUI, I wish that we'd had no early success whatsoever. Maybe then we would have passed that case on to someone else. It would prove toxic for us. In fact, it would be the Spymoms' poison pill.

Chapter 10

The Nude Professor

LIFE WAS GOOD—FAMILY LIFE AND WORK LIFE BOTH.
Jay was turning down promotions that would have meant leaving Boise. Christine was getting more serious about Ben; we adored him, and his parents had become our good friends. With the Christian school debacle behind him, Jeff had graduated from public high school and gone off to college in Twin Falls. Only Scott was still living at home. No one was pregnant or living in my basement. This was success, as I now defined it.

Actually, my kids were maturing into hardworking and faithful young people. Clients who were distraught over their children found it comforting to hear that mine were turning out okay. I could even make the case for rebellion at the appropriate age, because while both Jeff and Scott had their problems, when they came back, they had their own opinions and were stronger people for it.

The immediate threat of cancer had receded into the background again, but now I enjoyed the benefits of a lot of support. The campaign to raise money and national awareness had been so effective that it was much easier for people to relate: "Oh, you have breast cancer? My sister has breast cancer."

In fact, I had the disease of the decade. People were wearing pink and racing for the cure. "Survivor" had supplanted "victim" and "patient." My scars no longer meant that I'd gone five years without a recurrence; they meant I was alive. They were a badge of honor, a health care Purple Heart. It was as if I were a hero because I had a disease I'd had no choice about having. As if I were fighting the disease on behalf of other women, so they wouldn't get it.

I made good use of my survivor status. I had no scruples about moving to the head of a line or preboarding a plane. Before my hair grew in, I wouldn't hesitate to whip off my wig to throw investigation subjects off-balance.

I used it to get things for the kids. I wanted them to have PlayStation 2 the first Christmas it came out. When everyone was lining up outside the store, I caught the salesclerk as he was slipping in the back door. I said, "I know you can't do this, so I'm just putting this out there. I have cancer. I'm trying to buy a gift for my son, who is in remission from cancer." The salesclerk smiled. Then, I waited on line all night with the gamers. I treated them all to pizza, and they saved my place in line so I could take a break at one point. In the morning, when they handed out the seven sets, I got one.

Even my daughter used it. When she went to play tennis, she told the people assigning the courts, "I can't wait around to have a court. My mom has cancer." They actually gave it to her.

"I trained you so well." Tears of pride rose in my eyes.

The fact that cancer got all the attention was a little unfair to Mollie.

She was in a lot of pain and I felt just fine, but people were only interested in cancer. Most of the time, though, I told her to suck it up, because breast cancer was getting us a lot of things that we wouldn't have had otherwise. People paid attention.

She got that. "Work it, girl," She told me. "Work it."

Mollie's and my partnership was still thriving. We joked that we fit well as a unit because, while neither of us could sustain full-time work out in the job force, together we made one full-time person.

We each had things we preferred doing. She could stomach the custody cases, so she took the bulk of those. I testified in court more often, because I could stay cool and objective. We both liked the cheaters. There were a cluster of them coming at us. There was never any shortage of cheaters. It was satisfying to nail them.

One of my favorite cheater cases involved The Hardware Hunk. A young man contacted me because he'd gotten an anonymous call that said his girlfriend was cheating with a co-worker from her job at a Lowe's. All he knew was that the guy's name was Joe and that he was buff. Could we confirm and find out more?

I drove to the store and asked what department Joe worked in. I had no idea what tack I would take when I found him. Something would occur to me, I knew, because it always did. The cashier pointed me toward flooring.

I knew I needed some way to hold Joe's attention long enough to direct the conversation to the girlfriend, and I needed to document his answers. In the minute it took to walk to flooring, I decided what to do. I'd invoke my Hypothetical Husband. The HH was generally handy. He could be my fall guy when surveillance hit a snag, as in "Oh, officer, I'm sorry I'm parked here in this no parking zone, but I'm just waiting for my husband and he's a little late." Today, he'd be my reason to ask Joe a question and tape the answer.

There was no doubt about which one was Joe. He was the guy next to the stack of plywood, moving his arms in slow circles, shoulder height, to work his biceps. I'm no expert, but I'd say his biceps looked just fine. In fact, he was quite a specimen—over six feet of toned muscle, topped with chiseled features, ice-green eyes, and sun bleached hair. I immediately dubbed him the Hardware Hunk.

"Hi, Joe," I said. "I hear you're an expert in flooring, so I wanted to talk to you."

"Well, sure," he said. "What do you need?"

Hardware Hunk, meet Hypothetical Husband.

"I'm trying to get my husband to put down laminate," I said, "and I want him to do it himself. I know it's not that hard. You can show me how to do it, right? Thing is, he's out of town right now." I shook my head. "I can't drag him in here to even look at this stuff, so I'm going to videotape you showing me how and I'll play him the tape. Then, he won't have an excuse to say he can't do it."

"Well, sure," Joe said, reaching toward a roll of foam. "But let's start with the substrate."

"The what?" I said. I was busy centering him in the frame. It would be a shame to cut off that beautiful head.

"The laminate is floated over foam," he said, holding up a roll of greenish rubber. "Meaning it's not tacked down. First you remove your base molding with this." He held up a pry bar. "You make sure to mark where you took it from. Then roll out your underlayment." He grabbed a roll of foam and began unwrapping it. It took a bit of doing, so I grabbed the opening.

"Joe," I said. "You're such a good-looking guy. I've got a friend who'd be perfect for you. She's a math teacher, and she's got a *great* personality. She's so stable—"

"Oh," he said, focusing on the stubborn wrap, "thanks. But I'm kind of taken."

"Are you married? I mean, if it's all right to ask."

"No, but I have a girlfriend."

"Is it, you know, serious?"

"It's . . ." He didn't know how to characterize it. *It's a hot affair with another guy's girl, Joe*, I thought. *That's your category.*

"So, if you're not completely taken, you should consider my friend. She's a really decent, nice woman." Joe had wrestled the wrapping off and was unrolling the substrate. He picked up two pieces of the laminate.

"Some laminate has to be glued, but this kind of tongue-and-groove just has to be snapped together. And, you can take it apart and reposition it." He snapped and unsnapped just to show Hypothetical. "It's not hard to figure out. Should only take you about three or four hours. Just make sure you have the laminate run the same way the room does, because that makes the room look larger."

"You see, Bill," I said. "You see how easy this is. You can totally do this, Bill. Thanks to Joe, here." I kept the camera running.

"So what about my friend?" I asked nonchalantly. "I mean, seriously."

"No, no, no," Joe said. "I have a girlfriend. Really I do."

"My lady's a blonde. Is yours?" I was trying to get a description.

He put his head right into the noose. "Yes. She is a blond."

"Is she a weightlifter, like you?

"She's a runner. She runs five miles every day."

My stable teacher couldn't compete on this turf. I shifted course.

"My friend loves kids. In fact, she teaches Sunday School."

"Yeah, well. My girlfriend's a Christian and all like that."

"My lady's a pretty good dancer."

"We met on the dance floor."

"Oh really. So she likes to dance?" I knew the girlfriend in question was a dance instructor.

"She teaches people how to line dance. At the Five Points Casino."

Bingo.

I got him to describe the whole situation. He talked about her personality and how long they'd been going out, and what they liked to do, and how many times a week they got together. He got quite specific and detailed, because he didn't want to go out with my stable teacher with the good personality. When he had told me everything short of what they did in bed, I thanked him for all the flooring advice and left.

The problem was, I still didn't have his last name. I'd need a name to run a background check. I went to the customer service desk and told the clerk that kids were keying cars in the employees' parking lot. I went out and stood where I had a clear view of the lot.

In less than two minutes, the employee entrance was slammed open and all these guys came streaming out of the place and ran over to check out their vehicles. My guy ran to a black Dodge Ram. Now I would be able to run his plate. I found out his credit history and criminal background—everything my client might want to know.

It was a very satisfactory day's work. I would love it if I could resolve every case in a day and with as little angst. That's not how it goes.

Cheater cases weren't always so cut-and-dried though. I was once approached in the grocery store by a woman who recognized me from a

TV segment Mollie and I had taped for a local channel. My first impression was that Courtney looked like someone who'd have a housekeeper to shop for her. She was in her late fifties. Maybe early sixties. She was still beautiful in a classic way that never goes out of style. The flawlessly patrician profile. The custom suit and the strand of pearls. I'd bet her initials were monogrammed inside that lapel.

I immediately felt like Pitiful Pearl, a raggedy doll I'd had as a kid.

She had, she said in a discreet whisper, a teensy problem. Could we talk?

We made an appointment for the following week.

I went to her home to do the intake interview. Getting to Courtney's place meant a long drive up a private road. She and her husband lived in one of those houses clinging to the side of a mountain. It's the kind of place that immediately has me calculating how much it must have cost to haul all those bags of cement, those beams, boards, and nails up there. You'd either have to have a strong desire for a view or a terrific aversion to neighbors.

The house inside: Well. I'm always amazed when people choose to lay white carpeting. Casey, our Pyrenees, would make short work of that, I can tell you.

The walls held photos of Courtney's family at various ages and stages, arranged chronologically, it appeared. Surveying the walls left to right was sort of a time-lapse sprint through the decades of her life. A man—presumably her husband—appeared lithe on a tennis court, ardent in a tux next to Courtney's bridal white, at ease in an armchair, distinguished on the golf green.

Courtney sat on a couch that spanned the length of a two-story sheet of glass and told me her story. The tale was a long one, and the western sky, her backdrop, brightened to gold and dimmed to dusk while she described an idyllic childhood and a charmed adolescence. She'd married young and had two girls—two blonde beauties preserved in a formal studio portrait, who resurfaced along the wall as graceful, lacrosse-stick-wielding teens, then as graduates, in mortarboard, and finally as brides. Neither had ever caused any trouble, Courtney told me. Her very worst memory was of Ellie, her oldest, being wait-listed at Choate, an East Coast prep school.

Both sets of grandparents were alive and well. Even Skippy, the family spaniel of her children's youth, was alive and well.

Her husband, an investment banker who'd retired at fifty, was still attentive. In addition to the Idaho home near his family, they owned a condo in Costa Rica and a town house in Manhattan.

"I don't know," Courtney said, with a sigh. "I have everything that most people want. I'm not unhappy. I can't really justify this, to tell you the truth. Not really."

"So . . . then . . . ," I said, in that leading way I use when I want a client to get on with it. I couldn't take much more of her perfectly perfect life.

"All right." She laughed. "Here it is. The thing is, I want to find someone. An old boyfriend, 'the one that got away.' He's the only man I ever dated who rejected me. I suppose that's why he's still of interest."

She was married. She was beautiful. She was wealthy. Her husband was a hunk-and-a-half. But still, she wanted to reconnect with a man from her past. He was the most charming, most exciting man she'd ever dated, she said.

I couldn't help it. I asked, "What are you messing around for? Why re-establish an old relationship when you know if it ever got out, it would be very damaging? Very hurtful to your husband, if nothing else."

"I just want to know what happened to him," She smiled disarmingly. "I don't want more than that. I promise."

I felt myself warming to her. She didn't want a relationship with the guy after all. It was just a little curiosity, so what was the harm?

She set up a special e-mail address so that she and I could communicate.

It wasn't hard to find Ross Fraser. He was a tenured professor at a college in Oregon. Online, I found a paper he'd recently written for a symposium. His field was communications.

I called him and told him I was a graduate student in business communications. "I read your article and it is straight-on what I want to do for my thesis," I said. "Can I quote from it? I'll give you credit, of course. Can I ask you some questions? It's just a master's thesis, so it's not a superbig deal, but I want to make it as exciting and interesting as I can, and your article gave me *so* much information."

In short, I sucked up to him really thoroughly. I was just this twenty-eight-year-old graduate student who was so impressed with him.

That made two of us.

We e-mailed back and forth for a bit. Finally I called him and said, "You know what would really help? I know it's going to sound silly, but can I have a picture of you for my thesis? I don't have any pictures, and here you are, big expert, allowing me to use some of your information. That's going to look so good for *me*."

He was happy to send me a picture. Turned out he was a pretty good-looking man, in a professional, straight kind of way.

I got him to talk about his family.

"Oh, you're married?" I asked. "So you're married and you've got kids. So much for my chances."

I gave Courtney all the information I'd collected along with the photo. One day, she called me and said that she was going to contact him, just to see what happened. She wanted to know why he'd ditched her. She didn't want to jeopardize her marriage. She was only curious.

I wasn't sure what to advise her. Wasn't I supposed to be a neutral conduit of information?

When I found myself in a state of moral confusion, I would sometimes turn to my son, Jeff. One of the most striking things about him was the sure moral compass he seemed to possess. I called him late one Sunday night.

"I have a client who is about to do something so wrong, Jeff. I'm not sure what my role should be, whether to advise her or not. What do you think?"

"I can't tell you what to do," he said, "I know that if you saw someone standing at a cliff's edge—anyone, a stranger, even—you would pull him back." He paused, took a deep breath. "I guess, when all is said and done, it has to be your call. Follow your gut instinct."

The next day I called Courtney and told her, "Don't do it. You're going to be sorry."

"I have to speak with him," she said.

"Think of the problems you'll bring on if you do more than that. Even contacting him is probably over the line, as far as I'm concerned." I had acknowledged to myself that we weren't client and investigator, by that point. We'd become friends. I felt obligated to say what a friend would say. It didn't do any good.

A month went by and then I heard from Courtney again. She called and was quite excited because the professor had e-mailed her that he was very interested in meeting. If Courtney ever came to southern Oregon, he'd love to see her. He and his wife had an open relationship, and on and on. The whole bit.

"He's so nice," Courtney said. "He said, 'I always wondered what happened to you. I can't believe you came to find me!'"

When she made plans to go there, I warned her again. "Don't do it," I said. "You've got a husband. You've got kids you love and you've got grandkids. Don't do this thing."

By then, it was completely out of my hands.

If she had said at the start, "I'm going to use what you find out to wreck my life," I would have said, "Lots of luck, I'm not your PI." But the situation had evolved and her feelings had shifted, and now I didn't know what to do. I saw, if she did not, that she stood at the edge of a precipice, and I was acutely aware that I had helped her get there.

Courtney arranged a trip to Oregon with her husband. She was going to try to get away for a day. Before she finalized the arrangements, the professor asked for a picture of her, so she sent him a copy of a picture she'd sent me, sort of a Christmas picture. She was so beautiful that the photo looked like a glamor shot from *Town and Country*.

That really pushed him right over the edge. He called her and said, "Why don't I send you a more casual photo of myself?"

So she opened her e-mail and there was a picture of him in the nude. He was posed, reclining on a kind of Josephine couch, with one arm behind his head.

When she told me what he'd done, I said, "Oh my gosh. You are nuts if you do anything more with this guy."

He turned out to be a horrible slimeball and she had quite a time getting rid of him. She never did make the trip down there. I think what she really wanted was for him to say, "You were the only one in my life," so that she could say, "Well, too bad. You had your chance, chump." But she had been so intrigued by the situation that she had walked, step by step, toward disaster.

Fortunately, that photo cooled her obsession. I advised her to have someone come in and take the information off of her computer, which she did. What she didn't realize was that he could, at any point, contact her husband and forward some of her e-mails. It didn't go that way, though. The luck that had handed this woman a sunny life held.

In the more than six months since we'd concluded our formal contract, I had been her friend and sounding board. She couldn't tell anyone else, so I had served the important function of witness to her relationship. I had driven myself crazy advising her because I felt so responsible for a situation I had helped set in motion. I would have been better off collecting the information and handing it off to her—then averting my eyes.

Another time I crossed the line with a client, I was still working with Jan. We were keeping tabs on a woman, Audrey, for her soon-to-be-ex-husband. He had left because he was just sure she was cheating. Now, he was hoping we would find some dirt so that he could get custody of the kids.

Audrey made jewelry—really pretty amber necklaces and earrings. That's what got me in the door—I ordered jewelry from her. I visited and watched her cut and polish the yellow amber, chatting with her as she looped the chunks in wire and soldered the ends with a tiny soldering gun.

I came to genuinely enjoy her company and was happy to find that

her ex's accusations that she was involved with a drug-dealing boyfriend, or was in some other way a bad mom, were unfounded. She was
sweet with her kids, really loving. She didn't seem to have any dubious friends. She wasn't dating at all. Mollie did a thorough surveillance,
but Audrey just wore a path between home and the drycleaners, the
church, the kids' schools, Safeway, and Starbucks, where she met women
friends. She didn't go out clubbing. She didn't dispose of booze bottles.
Her phone records were unexceptional. No calls to drug dealers. No men
in her life. Nada.

In a way, I was not surprised, because we have found, over time,
that when guys suspect that their women are cheating, they are right
only sixty percent of the time. On the other hand, when a wife or girlfriend calls us because she's suspicious of her man, she's right a whop-
ping ninety percent of the time, even when he's telling her that she's
crazy and paranoid, or that she's going through menopause, or that she
must be the one who's cheating. In the other ten percent of cases, the
guy is up to *something*. As a consequence, we have a healthy respect for
women's intuition. There really seems to be something to that.

It took a while to figure out that Audrey was clean, though, and by
the time we wrapped up the investigation, I had enough jewelry for
everyone's birthday for the next year and for Christmas too.

I told Jan that I had decided to make Audrey a friend. She was someone I could genuinely relate to. Her husband was no longer my client, so
there was no real reason she couldn't be my woman friend, I thought.

But Jan pointed out that if I really wanted a genuine relationship with
Audrey, I would have to tell her that I had first approached her as part
of an investigation.

"How do you think she'll feel," Jan asked me, "when she learns that you were there under false pretenses to spy on her? That you were trying to find smut on her and get her kids taken away?"

Probably not too great.

Jan threatened to tell her if I did not. Ultimately, I dropped the whole idea.

We also had a soldier in Iraq who was a client and became a special friend. I still feel good about that case—how Mollie and I helped him, and how we stuck by him afterward. This young man contacted us because he had met a young lady in Boise on MySpace. She was, he told us, the love of his life.

She was a Latin beauty, the beloved only child of wealthy parents. She was earning a master's degree in engineering. He sent us an e-mail with her photo attached. She was, indeed, a sultry beauty.

They'd had a hot and heavy Internet correspondence over many months. At last, the time seemed right to come and meet her in person. The day he arrived, he got a message at his hotel. Unfortunately, her grandmother had died the day before. She had had to fly to Las Vegas and couldn't meet him.

He returned to Iraq, disappointed.

He then purchased, and had shipped to her, a computer hookup so that they could see each other while they chatted in real time.

She couldn't figure out how to hook it up, she told him. Then her computer crashed.

Even though the hookup hadn't worked out, he was still at least 80 percent sure that she was who she said she was. He was thinking that he wanted to propose to her, so he'd hired us to eradicate that last bit of doubt.

We got him to promise to wait until we'd at least had a little while to check her out before he bought a ring. We had him send flowers to her. He was pretty sure he knew her address. We followed the delivery to make sure that someone signed for the flowers.

After the flowers were delivered, we had him call her and ask if the flowers had arrived. She said yes and she thanked him. So then we knew we had the right person.

A while later, we came to the door and asked if she wanted to be part of a garage sale. We managed to get inside and saw that she had his picture up on the wall. He was standing there in his uniform, with his gun.

But she was not who she said she was. She was a little fourteen-year-old girl who thought it was pretty exciting stuff to have a boyfriend in Iraq. This was an undeveloped child, who certainly was no engineering student. Her parents weren't wealthy and she was no Latin beauty.

We had to get a picture so I said, "Oh, you have a what'cha-mah-call-it kind of dog. Can I take a picture for my husband? He loves those dogs." I took the picture of the dog and this girl before she had a chance to answer.

We e-mailed the photograph to our soldier. He called her and broke up with her, and she told him some sort of wild story. He was heart-broken. He'd never met her, but he was genuinely heartbroken. He had already planned his vacation to come and take her to visit his family in Las Vegas and they were going to stay at the Bellagio.

Then he spent hours and hours on MySpace trying to find the real person in the photograph, the Latin beauty, the woman he'd fallen in love with. When he found her, she wanted nothing to do with him.

It was just about unbearable, the lonely soldier in Iraq getting up at three in the morning so he could talk to her on the phone or by e-mail. I brought my upset home to Jay and he helped me by listening. When a case was especially upsetting, Jay was always there to talk me through it.

Mollie and I stayed in touch with our soldier. He stayed on in Iraq after his tour was up, working as a civilian. We both thought it was because he had nothing to come home for.

After a time, he came to understand that as awful as it was, it could have been worse. He could have gotten together with this fourteen-year-old without realizing she was underage and wound up in jail. We were like two mothers for him. Not that two mothers are any substitute for a gorgeous Latin beauty. Still, we were glad to be able to help—and knowing that we had genuinely made a difference for some people was what would keep me going when it all started going wrong.

Chapter 11

From Dancer to PI

NOT LONG AFTER THE END OF THE COURTNEY CAPER, I was approached at church by Tina Frederick, a new church member. She asked me to join her at Denny's for coffee. I accepted the invitation and sent Jay along home.

She sipped her coffee and I sucked down a Coke as her story emerged.

"A few days ago, I was driving with a friend of mine who'd just gotten out of prison," she said, "and we were, like, you know, we should be private investigators because we're so good at being bad, we would know how to catch them. And we laughed and I went, 'You know, that really isn't a bad idea.'"

Tina said right up front that she hadn't always been the good, upstanding Christian I saw before me. Some of her life experiences actually made her more fit for investigative work, she thought. "I think I'd be really good at chasing cheaters," she said. "The reason is, I've cheated every way possible, on every boyfriend I've ever had. And I've had more than my share of boyfriends, when you get down to it. I've had your share and Mollie's share too. I've dated enough musicians to form my own band. Twice."

Tina was a statuesque blonde in her late thirties, who certainly looked fit and tough. She didn't look like she'd need to pack a stun gun. She also had other qualifications that I wouldn't find out until later on—like, she was on the way to an associate degree in criminology, with her eye on a master's.

As Tina told me about her background, it occurred to me that she would be able to go places this soccer mom could not. Tina recounted a strong Mormon upbringing and how she had rebelled. She had fallen away from her faith after an older sister filled her in on the role of polygamy in early Mormonism.

By the time she turned nineteen, Tina had two marriages behind her and two sons to raise. She hated being on welfare, so she studied accounting in order to become a bookkeeper. When bookkeeping didn't bring in enough, she also became an exotic dancer—an exotic dancer in a bikini, not a stripper. Both of Boise's bikini bars—Norm's Inn and the Kit Kat Klub—had a rule that customers couldn't get any closer than six inches, or the length of a dollar bill, to the dancers.

"It was the most fun I ever had," Tina told me, "and I was in such awesome shape. I loved the dancing. I loved the presents. I loved when they would call my name to go up on stage and everybody in the crowd just went absolutely wild. And, when you finished your routine, there would be a standing ovation, and they'd be screaming and pounding on the tables. It was such a rush.

"I didn't always make the most money, but I always got the most presents and I always got more applause than anybody. I was really into the choreography and my music."

Tina called on a family friend to take care of her boys while she danced.

"I called One-legged Jay, in California," she told me. "'I need someone to help me with the boys because I'm working two jobs,' I said. 'Come on up to Idaho. I'll pay you $300 a week.' He wasn't sure, so I told him, 'Jay, I work as an exotic dancer in a club. I'll get you in.' He didn't need more convincing than that. So he became our nanny-Mr. Belvedere."

The Boise clubs were eventually shut down, so she danced in nearby Caldwell. Tina loved finding dope in the wadded up dollar bills men gave her. She got more teeners and eight balls of coke and crank than she could do, even partying all night and pushing the envelope to find what her limit was. She would wind up giving a lot of it away.

She drove call girls from a strip club to their appointments on behalf of her boyfriend, their boss. She waited outside in the car and timed the session. Then she would call the girl from her cell phone and say, "Tell the john his hour's up unless he wants to pay more."

Four years later, Tina had turned her life around. She was clean and sober, her life sustained by belief and her church family. She eventually became a trusted member of our team.

For her debut Hanady case, Tina worked with me to investigate a cheater.

Our client was a man from Baker, a little mountain town on the Idaho-Montana border. He was upset, he said, because his decade-long affair had cooled. He was afraid his girlfriend had a new love interest.

Tina and I drove to Baker to meet our prospective client, Allan, at a local eatery. He was a handsome and distinguished-looking man who appeared to be in his early sixties. He'd thoughtfully brought a picture of his honey. She was a nice-looking woman. No youngster.

"She's been the best," he said. "Ten years. I can't believe she's stepping out on me with someone else."

"You mean, someone else besides her husband," I said, just to keep track.

"Yes." He sighed. "When I hit eighty, I slowed down some. Only once a day. Maybe that was a turnoff for her."

I can't speak for Tina, but I can tell you I was dumfounded. What was this man's secret? I was trying to think of a tactful way to ask.

Allan slid an envelope with money toward us. Tina, who had made a move to pick it up, paused.

"I just have to know," she said. "Can I ask you a personal question?"

He nodded.

"You're eighty."

"Yes." He nodded.

"And everything still works?"

"Yes."

"And it's still good?"

"It's just gets better as you get older," he said. "You're not doing backflips like when you were twenty, but it's good."

"Why aren't you out chasing thirty-year-olds?" I asked.

"Well, they're okay for a good time," he said, "but you really can't have a conversation. I like my women to be sixty-five, seventy. There's nothing like a nice bottom."

For a moment I was tempted to work pro bono just for this man's enlightened worldview.

Tina and I did surveillance together for this case.

His lady friend was a Realtor, so we parked in a lot next to her office. The lot belonged to a store that made the surveillance less boring than the usual. It was a little store covered with signs that offered bait, tackle, beer, ice, whatever. But they also had a drive-through window, and a pretty steady stream of cars kept pulling up. We were thinking that maybe they were selling something more than produce. We decided to go and check this out. We found fishing poles, canoes, ice hammers, eggs and lettuce. We also discovered that they had a fountain and a deli. They had worms in the refrigerator. Pretty much anything you could ever want. The cashier was a country guy in denim overalls and old flannel.

I grabbed a Coke and Tina nabbed one too. She asked the cashier, "So. What do you guys sell through the window?"

"Anything."

"Anything?"

"Yup. As long as it fits through the winder. Fishing poles. Tackle. Yup. Once tried to sell a feller an augur through that winder. Stuck."

We got to know all the store guys pretty well, because Allan's lady friend didn't do anything much except talk on the phone and meet with people who looked like legitimate clients.

After a week of this, we got back to Allan. We didn't have anything substantial to report and he seemed a little crestfallen.

Tina said, "You know, she might have quit fooling around because she hit that age in her life when you slow down. You're not really the norm. You're more of a phenomenon, as a daily eighty-year-old."

"Things are going from bad to worse," he said, burying his head in his hands. "Now all she does is quote Scripture."

"Was she always a big Bible reader?" I asked, "Or is that something different for her?"

"Well. Now that you mention it, she used to read those romance novels, but now she keeps a Bible on the nightstand."

"She might be having some guilt because she's having an affair," I said. "It might have caught up with her."

Ultimately we all agreed that she wasn't cheating; she was feeling remorse. We decided that he needed to leave it alone and find someone else—and no more married women.

Mollie called Tina one night when we needed someone to tail our old friend Monique. Monique was going out to a particular restaurant, and Mollie suggested that Tina follow her in and see what she could find out.

"I stood at the bar and ordered a drink," Tina told me afterward. "I watched them for a while, and then I decided, 'What the heck.' I took out my little camera and walked over to their table. I said, 'I'm really sorry to interrupt you guys, but I got stood up on a date tonight, and he's, like, a miserable slob. I just want him to know I didn't sit home alone tonight. So if I buy you a drink, would you take a picture of me with your boyfriend?' Monique was like, 'Okay. Sure.'

"We talked about men and what dirtbags they are and getting older and turning forty and how much that stinks. She told me that she had an ex who was messing with her and her child. And wouldn't you know it, it so happened I had an ex who was doing the same thing." Tina laughed. "I was commiserating."

Tina got Monique to tell her about their plans to go out to Murphy's for her birthday. Tina actually sat there at the bar with the recorder in her hand, taping the whole thing, because they were so oblivious. Monique told her that she'd twisted the arm of her older daughter to watch the younger one so she could go out to celebrate her birthday.

Of course, that was what we were listening for. That was illegal. Monique wasn't supposed to leave the little girl with anyone else, so Tina followed Monique when she went out on her birthday, and we got her on contempt.

Monique would drink herself into oblivion and drive home. That was her pattern. It was happening over and over. We'd get her on contempt or we'd get her for yet another DUI and for losing her license. The court would grant Grandma emergency custody and then send the child back to that so-called mother.

One time I called Tina when we needed some surveillance. I threw her right into another infidelity case. A guy had called, pretty sure his wife and his friend were doing the deed. His wife had a day off coming up and he wanted us to follow her. Fortunately, Tina lives just a few subdivisions away from this guy, so when he called, she could get right in place and wait. She kept her cell phone on, so I could talk her through it, if need be.

Tina was ready when his wife got in the car that morning and drove, with their little boy, to Starbucks. Tina followed her inside. The wife took a table. Tina sat behind her, in an armchair.

An elderly gentleman joined the wife. Tina heard the man, who had to be the kid's grandfather, promise the little boy a day at the swimming pool. Grandpa left with the child and the wife drove off, with Tina tailing. The wife drove through a carwash, then she parked at a McDonald's. She got into a truck with some guy and they took off. Tina had the presence of mind to memorize the license plate in case she lost them.

She called me on her cell. "I can't believe this, what a rush." She said, excitement coloring her voice. "I've got, like, ten points on my driving record, and I don't want to tell you how fast I'm going to keep up with them. And, you know, I might as well have a neon sign over the car that says, "I am FOLLOWING you."

"Hang in, Tina." I laughed. "And please be careful." Boise is like Truck Driver Central, with all the products and goods that come here. There are always multiple freight lines on the freeway, and Tina was zipping in and out between them.

"I'm praying, 'Don't let me be killed,' you bet I am."

I was cheering her on. She was doing great. Couldn't be better.

They all exited the freeway and headed up to Lucky Peak. I told Tina to stay well behind, because traffic thinned out on that road. The road wound up the steep incline and Tina took the turnoff to Spring Shores, thinking they were there, but they weren't. They must have headed up to Arrow Rock, she decided.

Ten fingernail-biting minutes later, she called me. "I went up to Arrow Rock and guess what?" she said.

"Don't make me guess," I said. "I hate that."

"I went on up to Arrow Point and I flipped around the corner and there was his truck, parked down below, in the sand. And guess what?"

"Don't *do* that."

"I had the clearest, best view of them in the truck bed. And after, they went skinny-dipping in the lake. That zoom feature on your camera really is state of the art."

Tina broke off our conversation to call the client. She told him, "Go ahead and clean out your bank account because she is cheating on you."

He wanted to know if it was the friend he had suspected. Tina went to the DMV and ran the plates, then called him back and confirmed that he was right.

Tina told him that his wife's car was still in the McDonald's lot and she would have to go back there to pick it up. He asked Tina to pick him up and wait there with him. In the meantime, he called his friend's wife, and according to Tina, said, "Do you know your husband and my wife are up at Lucky Peak right now and they're having an affair?"

His friend's wife was shocked, because she had just had a baby six months before. She came down, too, and all three of them waited across the street for the lovers to return.

Then, Tina told me, our gal cheater called her husband. "I've been trying to get hold of you." She said, "Where have you been?"

"That's a secret," He answered.

"A secret? What do you mean?"

"Well, your birthday's coming up soon. . . ."

She bought it. *Happy, happy birthday, baby.*

So the truck pulled into the parking lot a little while later and both of them got out. Our client's wife was oblivious, but her lover saw his wife coming and jumped back in the truck and put the pedal to the floor, while she ran after the truck, screaming at him.

Our cheater gal tried to get in her car, but our client grabbed the car keys and slammed the door shut. Then, her cell phone rang. It was her lover, calling to get their stories straight.

Her husband grabbed the phone and played it to the hilt. He told the so-called friend that he had had an investigator following them all day. There was a videotape, and unless they came clean, he was going to view the tape.

His wife spilled her guts. She told him everything.

The next day, the client called Tina and told her about his tearful conversation with his wife. She was full of excuses and he didn't know what to do. Tina told the client, "Just wait. Next she'll tell you that it's your fault because you accused her so much that she figured she might as well just go ahead and do it." He called back in two hours. Sure enough, that's what his wife had said, almost word for word.

I cautioned her not to let him see the pix if there was any chance to save their marriage.

I always asked clients, "Do you really want to see pictures? It's one thing to know. It's another thing to see. Do you really want to open that envelope?"

And if they said, "Yes, I need to be absolutely sure. I need to confirm with my own eyes," my heart would kind of sink, because once those photos are burned into heart and mind, there is no way to remove them.

Tina resolved that case in a way that would become her trademark. When the client asked her what she thought he should do about the relationship, she told him that he wouldn't be less of a man if he decided to take her back.

"You're not wussin' out," she said. "It takes a strong man to be able to forgive." Marriages could be healed, she said, even in the worst of circumstances. Her own marriage was just that kind of a miracle. She told him about the support she had gotten from her church community. She gave him information about Christian couples counseling. I don't know what ended up happening with that couple, but I do know that we had made the right decision in bringing Tina on board.

Chapter 12

In the Corn Maze

ONE TIME WE WERE WORKING ON A CHEATER CASE and we knew it was the perfect opportunity for our junior investigators—Maddie, Cate and Alison—to help us out. On a bright, clear fall day, we loaded up the car and headed to the Corn Maze. Our cheater guy ran the maze and we expected that his honey would turn up that day. We knew the girls could help us catch them on film and the girls could have a little fun while they were at it. Also, we knew they'd be safe. We had thoroughly vetted both the principals with an extensive background check, so we were sure that the day's sleuthing would not endanger our junior PIs.

We didn't tell them where we were headed, though, and the Juniors kept trying to get Mollie to spill it. "Is it a custody case? they asked. "Is it insurance fraud? Or is it a cheater?" They hoped it was a cheater because they were the most fun.

"Cool your jets," Mollie kept saying. "You'll just have to wait and see. It won't be long."

But on the way to the site, we spotted Monique's unlicensed daughter driving her car. It was a real break. We made a detour and turned to follow her, hoping to document that the little girl was with her. I turned into the mall's east entrance at the next light, trailing a few cars behind the girl.

The Junior Investigators in my back seat suddenly came to life. "The mall!" Alison shrieked.

"Oh, we won't make you go into the mall," Mollie said. "We know you guys would rather just wait in the car—"

"*No-o-o . . .*"

I had to smile at the predictable chorus of groans.

"We can't just, like, let her disappear," Maddie said. "I mean, we have to go in there and find her."

We made a slow circle through the lot, looking for the bright blue car. We didn't see it, but Mollie wanted to go inside and search.

"I just think she's in there. I want a photograph of her with Shirleen," Mollie said. "Actually, what we need is a photograph of her putting Shirleen in the car, because that's the legal issue. Otherwise, Mom could have dropped them both off at the mall, you know?"

I could see that Mollie was adamant. I was inclined to cut her slack, because I knew that she was in more pain than usual. When she's in a psoriatic flare, her immune system misfires and starts attacking her body and it's anybody's guess where it will happen next. Kidneys, teeth, eyes, ankles, joints—any body part. I knew that today she felt like damaged goods, like a defective item that should be plucked from the conveyor belt and thrown in a pile.

I wasn't sure it was a good idea to go inside and look around, but I'd be happy enough to trade the heat for a blast of air conditioning. "All right," I said, as we all headed for the mall entrance. "What's the game plan, Molls?"

"I say we start here at the north end and work our way south. If we see her, you and I will hang back and let the girls shadow.

"Yay, we can window-shop," Maddie and the girls said.

"No, ladies." I had to be the bad guy. "This is a job. Sorry." I gauged them for the pout factor. Cate and Alison might have been on the verge of sullen, but not Maddie. She was a pro. She put an arm over the shoulder of each girl and gave them a little shake. "Smi-i-ile. It's a-a-all good." Good little junior sleuth.

But where was Mollie? I turned around and found her two stores back, staring, transfixed, into Victoria's Secret. I went back to her.

"Look, there's the cutest, cutest, cutest pair of pants. They don't usually have pants."

"No window-shopping, Mom," Maddie said.

The two-story mall, with more than one hundred stores, was your basic zoo. The whole of Ada County seemed to be there to escape the heat. I saw baby carriages so loaded with packages that you had to look twice to find the baby. I saw multiple teens, dressed so alike they could have been issued uniforms at the mall entrance. The uniform was baggy pants, showing lots of boring boxers. If I have to look at boxers, they should at least have a fun print. "What do you think about those?" I elbowed Maddie, who said, "Yuck."

We worked our way through the mall, methodically, Mollie limping along. We walked through the top floor to the south, then went down a level and worked our way back north. It took about an hour to look through every store. Near where we had first come in, we collapsed onto benches.

"I'm done," I said. "That's it. They're not here."

"I'm going through one more time." Mollie's jaw was set. "We didn't check the restaurants. They could have been in a restroom."

Dang, I was frustrated. We were wasting a perfectly good Saturday morning.

"Not to be blunt or anything, but this is a little bit nuts, Mollie," I said. "It's time to fold 'em. We'll be in the food court."

We straggled toward the food. I remembered that we had passed a Hallmark Creations store near the entrance. I decided to duck inside, because I was on the lookout for a specific greeting card a client had asked me to find.

Unfortunately, I got distracted by a toy store we had to pass along the way. It had a massive display of stuffed bunnies in the window.

Maddie looked at me and smiled. "Double dog dare you."

I was already on it, headed for the bunnies. Maddie knew I would always take a dare to mess with a store display. It was goofy fun and I could get away with it, because I had on my cloak of invisibility.

I took all the sunglasses from one display and put them all on the stuffed bunnies in the other. The girls stood in a little knot outside the store, whispering and giggling. Objectively, I thought the display looked quite a bit better when I was done. The rabbits were stylin'.

Inside Hallmark, I scanned the racks while the girls thumbed through the birthday cards. I needed a card featuring Winnie the Pooh for a new case. We'd been contacted by an attorney in London on behalf of a client. She wanted us to check out her Internet love interest, a local Idaho fellow, before she flew over to meet him. We were to purchase a Winnie the Pooh card for this man's birthday, inscribe it with a specific poem, and mail it to him to arrive exactly on his birthday.

I thought we could save her time, money and probably heartache by telling her he was a fake and a liar. A forty-seven-year-old guy who loves Winnie the Pooh? That should have been her first clue. But they never listen.

After we found the card, we went to the food court. The girls opted for cheeseburgers. I loaded my tray with the usual grilled cheese sandwich, french fries, and a chocolate shake. I used to eat more healthy food before cancer, but now I eat what I want. For me, the six food groups are pizza, fries, chocolate shake, grilled cheese, Coke, and anything peppermint.

We'd been there less than five minutes when Mollie appeared, her limp more pronounced. Her house salad looked tiny on the empty tray.

She picked at the lettuce.

I said, in a mock-dramatic aside to the teens, "She's getting fat. We don't like to tell her, but . . . she's really getting fat." At the same time, I speared one of her three lettuce leaves. I always eat off her plate and she filches food from mine.

"Don't eat it all."

"Why ever not? You don't want it. I need to keep up my strength because—"

Everyone joined me on the chorus: "I have *cancer*."

But we couldn't tease Mollie into eating.

We emerged from our air conditioned haven to find we were shriveling under the kind of relentless sun and dry heat that is the Boise standard. The car seemed like it was ten miles away.

"I want a disability sticker so we can park closer," I said, joking but not really. "I should be able to get anything I want."

We piled back into the car and headed to the corn maze. Cornfields cut into giant mazes are a popular attraction in Idaho. You can spend hours turning in circles along miles of paths. There are even haunted mazes with real live ghosts to make it scary fun. Many of the mazes are cut into designs.

Our destination maze had featured the BSU Broncos logo last year. If we could believe the brochure, this year's offering was even more intricate: a replica of the Great Seal of the State of Idaho, featuring a miner with pick and shovel, an elk head, a goddess, a sheaf of wheat, several horns of plenty, and an unfolding vista of the Snake River, over which floats Idaho's official motto, *Esto Perpetua*, which means something like "It goes on forever." That seems just right for this five-acre maze, with its three miles of trails.

To me, the designs always seemed like an insane amount of work. The thing is, unless you have an aerial view, you can't tell what it is, anyway. From the ground, it just looks like a big field of corn. But people here love them. The teens love them. Cate and Alison were bouncing like little kids in the back when we pulled up to the maze. Maddie, however, was looking around, making a mental checklist of everything in the vicinity.

We had trained our junior investigator well. Mollie and I exchanged a look.

"Yes, she's totally cool," I admitted.

Our subject was a trim man in his forties. He wore a polo shirt and loafers that clashed with his farmer-style hat and the long stalk of grass he chewed on. He was absorbed in an animated discussion with a raven-haired beauty.

Mollie explained the objective—the girls were to film each other, making sure that they had the cheater and his girlfriend in focus in the background. We didn't want them alerted to the surveillance, she cautioned them. They had to look like teen girls just out for a fun time in the corn maze. They shouldn't just hang in the vicinity of their subjects. But they shouldn't forget that that's what they were there for.

"Leave everything to us," Maddie said confidently. "I've watched you do this for years."

I took Mollie by the arm.

"Come on, Mom. Let's go for a walk. They're going to be just fine."

We entered the maze. The paths were wide enough for two to walk abreast. The stalks, at ten feet, towered over us. The cornstalks rustled. Otherwise it was quiet. It smelled green. We came upon a little clearing where someone had thoughtfully placed a pair of white plastic chairs, so we sat down, shaded by the tall plants.

We fanned ourselves with our maze maps and we talked a little business, in a just-passing-time sort of way. Then I started remembering something that was bothering me. I'd meant to bring it up, but I kept forgetting. It was about surveillance.

"I feel like I'm handing off too much surveillance to you," I said. "Plus the custody cases. Grandma and Monique, especially. I go, 'You could take over this part of it and do this because' —I dropped my voice to a confidential whisper—'I hate to bring this up, but I've got *cancer*. And I just think, you know, that's all I can handle.' Which leaves you with all the hard stuff. Meanwhile, you're suffering more than I am. Why do I keep being allowed to say that when you know I'm using it? Why do you let me do that?"

Mollie looked up from her cell phone. She had begun fiddling with it when I opened this subject. She said, "I'm a huge enabler."

"But why *do* you let me keep doing that?"

"I'm less codependent now. I read *Codependent No More*. I need to read it again."

I thought she was taking on too much, I really did. If she only dropped Grandma and Monique, just that alone would be a big load off. Watching her look for Shirleen and the daughter in the mall had really clinched it for me.

"I know you want me to drop Grandma," she said, mindreading or whatever it was that she did. "I just keep thinking about that little girl. I can't forget about her."

"I want us to be out from under this one," I said. "I think this case is just killing you."

Mollie's phone rang. It was her son, asking where she put his medication.

Mollie's phone rang again. It was Kellin again, asking what time she would pick him up. Then she was tickety-tick-tapping on the thing.

"Now what?"

"I'm texting my kids. One daughter says thank you for the money. One daughter is asking me what I'm doing."

"You can't text and surveil at the same time."

"I'm multitasking. Welcome to the twenty-first century."

"I can't multitask. And it's rude not to look at someone when you're talking to them."

She looked up at me, mock-mortified.

"Oh, Valerie, I'm so sorry. I apologize profusely. Zillions of times over. You're the best, you're the greatest, you're the most beautiful—"

"Everything you say is so *true*," I said, punctuating the sentence by reaching over and grabbing the darned phone.

Mollie grabbed it back and started looking at photos. She passed me a picture of a pug dog, of her kids costumed in stuffed bras.

"They're cute, they're adorable," I said. "They're not the problem. The problem is that you're calling this thing your *precious*."

Mollie turned the thing on me and took my photograph.

"What are you going to do now? Post me on the Internet?"

I guess we sat there for an hour. Maybe a little less. As we walked toward the gate we'd come in, I heard squeals and laughter I recognized. There were our intrepid trio, giggling like silly thirteen-year-olds while they posed and took turns videotaping each other. Behind them—but close enough to be in focus—cheater and girlfriend grappled in a serious-looking clinch.

I wanted to tell the kids to wait until they were done kissing so they get a clear shot of her face, but I needn't have worried. When I saw the beautiful footage our juniors got, I knew that Mollie and I could not have done better.

It was great for their self-esteem, Mollie said, and one more step toward letting them be investigators, not just members of an investigators club.

We turned them loose in the corn maze after that and topped that with a blowout at Baskin-Robbins.

Chapter 13
The Wonder of It All

JEFF CALLED TO SAY HE WAS COMING HOME FROM college for a visit. He was bringing a friend with him. A girl. I braced myself.

Right away, I could tell that Tia was a lot of energy in a small package. She was tiny, blonde and bubbly. She was very, very young. She wore a vinyl cap shaped like a train engineer's, boots, a tiny skirt with oversized daisies, hoop earrings and a Halloween-themed manicure I later learned she'd done herself.

My family likes to play board games, and Tia and Jeff jumped into a game of Pictionary. The teams were Jeff, Tia and me, against Christine, Christine's boyfriend Ben, and Jay. The other team picked a card, and Jay—their artist—did a drawing to convey the concept to his teammates without using words. Before Christine and Ben could open their mouths to guess what the drawing was, Tia forgot herself and said, "Oh, it's a dog. A sleeping dog!" She completely gave away the answer to their team. I dinged her on the head with a pencil. She looked completely shocked. In fact, it wasn't a bad initiation into the ways of Family Agosta. Games are serious business. Whether it was Pictionary, Racko, foosball, pool, air hockey, or Ping-Pong, I played to win.

Between rounds, we learned a little about Jeff's new girlfriend.

Tia had lived all her life in Twin Falls, which is a town of about thirty thousand, an hour outside of Boise. She had four siblings and her parents ran a restaurant together. Her mom and dad loved NASCAR races.

"So," I said, when I had a chance to speak with Jeff alone, "when did you guys get together? How'd you meet?"

"We met over Christmas," Jeff said.

"We've been dating since December 31," Tia, who'd overheard us, added. "Are there 31 days in December? I can sing you the song," and she did, clapping to the schoolyard ditty, "There are seven days, there are seven days, there are seven days in the week . . ."

Tia and Jeff had met through Tia's roommate, who had had a crush on Jeff. Tia had not been terrifically impressed with Jeff at first sight. She didn't like his long hair and the fact that he always wore a hat, even in church. He was skinny and he smoked cigarettes.

After they started dating, she got him to cut his hair and clean up his act.

"The smoking goes," she told him.

When I heard that, I thought, *Well, good for you. I've never been able to get him to do that.*

I was also impressed as heck when Jeff told me that Tia had, by the time she graduated from high school, socked away thirteen thousand dollars in a savings account. She had worked three jobs through high school.

We had met other girls Jeff had dated through the years, but this relationship was different, we could all tell. Still, they were both young. They had time to take it easy, like Christine and Ben, who had been dating seriously for two years and were moving toward marriage, but on a self-prescribed "slow track."

A few weeks later, he came down from school and again brought Tia. She was wearing a promise ring, a pre-engagement token.

A month later, Tia was wearing an engagement ring.

"No time soon, Mom," Jeff said, before they'd even taken off their coats.

So of course they were married within the year, in August 2005. At the wedding shower, she got me back for the pencil ding by putting me in a headlock and giving me a noogie. Her mom was quite taken aback by the extreme informality of it all.

Getting together with Tia was one of the wisest decisions Jeff ever made. Just below that bubbly surface is a reservoir of character and grit. She is for Jeff, first and last, and he is for her.

In fact, she's so on top of things she can be a little scary. Tia was a substitute grade school teacher in Twin Falls. The kids loved her to death and she was really tough on them too. Once, I had to call her during the school day. I hated to have the phone call in the middle of her teaching. "I'm sorry, I don't want to interrupt your class," I said.

"Wait a minute," she said. "Hang on." I could hear her talking to the kids, "What is Mrs. Agosta holding in her hand? And when she has a phone in her hand, what do we all do?"

And suddenly the room was silent, I said, "I'm afraid to talk to you."

Everything is fresh and new to Tia. Through her, we get the chance to see things that have become so familiar that we just don't see them anymore.

We all took a trip to Ocean Shores. It was the first time she had seen the ocean. She was thrilled by the thunderous, rolling combers, the broad reach of sand. She made us see the wonder of it all with her enthusiasm.

She's also very straightforward and spontaneous. She says what's on her mind.

Tia trained as a nail tech and found a job doing manicures and pedicures. The first time she did a pedicure on a transvestite, she had no idea what the score was until she glanced up between those legs widespread in traditional male stance.

She called me. I couldn't, for the life of me, hear what she was going on about. She was whispering Tammy's a *guy*. She's a *guy*. I asked her several times to repeat herself.

Tia thought the problem was that I didn't grasp the concept, that this alleged female was really male. She yelled at the top of lungs, so loud that she must have been audible clear to the street, "Tammy's a DUDE."

It wasn't long after that, that Tia joined me on a case. I didn't realize it, but Tia had been a little nervous about my PI work. She was afraid that I would investigate her—not that she had any deep, dark secrets to uncover.

She came along over Jeff's objections. He thinks my job is crazy. I think he is a little overprotective, but there is a reason for it. Tia was once in a serious car crash. A truck smashed into the back of her vehicle, slamming Tia's car into the truck ahead of her. The effect of the double whiplash was to displace part of her brain. Fifteen centimeters slipped toward her neck, putting pressure on the spinal cord. The displacement, called a Chiari Malformation, prevents the free flow of cerebral fluid. Fortunately for Tia, a little fluid does get through. If it did not, she would be paralyzed. But her CM also gives her headaches.

She had a headache when I picked her up in Twin Falls for our first case. We were driving to nearby Filer, the tiny town where our subject lived. Despite her pain, Tia was her bubbly self. She climbed into my car and leaned across the seat to give me a hug. "Hi, Mom," she said. She calls me Mom. She winced a little as she slammed the car door. "My head. It's pulsating so bad. That doctor keeps trying to give me morphine, Vicodin and Valium, but I won't take them because I hate pills."

"I did look at those CM Web sites," I said. "There's an operation that they sometimes do."

"Oh, Jeff and I talked to the doctor about that. They cut a part of your brain off and put a shunt up there, in your cerebellum, so the fluid can flow. Jeff said to him, 'How do you know what part of the brain you're cutting off? What if that's her love or her emotions?'"

Tia would rather live with it, she decided. It was manageable. Anyway, the only pain that really scared her was the pain of childbirth. She had already decided she would opt for every kind of pill there was when the time came. I promised to make them give her every drug in the book.

Our subject today was a woman who was engaged to marry Mike, a man quite a bit older than she. Mike's parents had hired us to check her out. Was she who she said she was? Was she after Mike's money?

We pulled up in front of her house. It was way out in the country. Everything in Filer is, by definition, out in the country. I told Tia that I was going to use my "little old lady" persona, and all she had to do was follow my lead. It would be fun.

So Tia knocked on the door with me and did her first pretext. All I had to do was say to the woman who answered the door, "Hi, we're new to the neighborhood," and Tia was off and running.

"Can you tell me about the schools here?" she said. "My kids have been home-schooled, but I think they should go to public school here so they get to know kids. Oh, do you have kids? Oh gosh, how old are they?"

That was smart, because one of the things I had been asked to find out was whether her kids were the same ages she had told her fiance's parents they were.

We chatted for about twenty minutes and then we left. When we got back to Twin Falls, I realized I had forgotten to take photos of the woman's license plate. I wanted to make sure she really did come from Arizona, as she'd told her fiance.

I put on a different wig, and we left my car and picked up Tia's 4Runner. I hoped that the woman wouldn't recognize us. I was in front of the house, leaning out of the car window, snapping pictures, when Tia said, "Mom. Put your camera down, she's looking at you." The woman was indeed peering out the front window, watching us.

Then Tia took the lead. She said, "We have to go back and knock on the door and tell them a story so they don't get suspicious."

The woman opened the door when we knocked, but just a crack this time. She peered out at me and I thought, *What if she thinks it's weird that I have different hair?* But if she did, she didn't say anything.

"Oh my gosh," Tia said, "We didn't mean to scare you. We just wanted some pictures of this beautiful house, because we want to build one kind of like it when we move to this neighborhood." There was development under way not far from the woman's house, so the story seemed plausible enough.

"I'm Elaine," the woman said and opened the door. "I'm sorry. I really should have introduced myself before. Won't you come in?"

Tia's talent for small talk soon had our hostess showing us the family albums. This story had a happy ending, because it became clear that Elaine was who she said she was. She and Mike did marry, and for all I know, lived happily ever after.

Not long after that, Tia stopped by just as I was getting ready to install a minicam for a case. She asked to come along.

Mollie and her daughter met up with us outside our client's apartment building. Our client was out of town and her boyfriend had threatened to break in while she was away. We were to install a secret camera in the apartment, so that if he really was intent on robbing her, we could catch him.

I had my stun gun, just in case.

We had several flights of stairs to climb, because our client had the apartment on the top floor. I taught the girls how to get up stairs without making them creak. We went up on all fours to distribute the weight, placing our feet and hands away from the middle of the stairs to avoid the creakiest worn spots.

I imagine we provided some amusement to the building residents who passed us on the stairs.

Once inside the apartment, we looked for a strategic spot to place the camera. Our client had suggested we place it in a Mickey Mouse. She hadn't mentioned how extensive her collection was. It was a little disconcerting to flip on the light and find hundreds of little eyes staring at us.

We chose a Mickey attached to a lamp and I installed the camera in the black ears. Mollie tried to get the VCR to work and couldn't. I tried to get it to work too.

Then we heard stairs creaking. Someone was on his way up to the apartment. Everyone except me ran screaming into a closet. Tia actually ran into a wall with a whomp that was as good as announcing "Here we are," and I heard her wail, "I chipped my wedding band."

Mollie hissed, "Get in here, hide, it's a bad guy!" and pulled her into the closet.

I planted myself in front of the closet door, stun gun at the ready. Everything was quiet. I could see feet blocking the light under the apartment door.

It seemed like forever until whoever it was retreated. I heard the deliberate tread of a big man going down the stairs. I whipped open the closet door and there were Maddie and Tia, completely buried under a pile of clothes with just the tips of their sneakers sticking out, and Mollie, posed like a bodybuilder with the client's 38 DD Wonder Bra on over her Junior-Petite sweater.

Chapter 14

Walnuts, Pine Nuts and Just Plain Nuts

SOMETIMES SLEUTHING COULD BE ITS OWN LITTLE slippery slope. We soon discovered that it was possible to slide so far into a case that we found ourselves making poor decisions in pursuit of the truth.

We got an insurance fraud case in Pocatello, in southeast Idaho, the part of the state originally settled by Mormons. The man being investigated had been driving when he was hit from behind. The accident was a minor fender-bender, but he was asking Prudential for ninety thousand dollars. He could barely raise his arms from his sides, he said. He couldn't lift ten pounds. He needed surgery.

Prudential's attorney gave us his medical records to look over. The file revealed that he had ankylosing spondylitis, the same inflammatory arthritis fusing Mollie's spine and sacroiliac joints. He might well need surgery, but his condition had nothing to do with the accident. It was clear he was just trying to pass those costs along to someone else.

Mollie and I drove to his home in Pocatello. Once we were outside his house, I realized that we couldn't do car surveillance, because there was no cover.

I said, "We have to knock on the door. That's the only way we're going to know if he's there. If he is, we need to get him talking in some kind of animated way, so that we can see if he has mobility in his arms."

We were arguing as we went up the walk. I wanted to use Estate Sale, but Mollie didn't think they would believe us.

I scrambled the numbers of his home address and wrote that number on a piece of paper. I opened the Pocatello newspaper to the estate sale section and tucked it under my arm. As soon as we rang the bell, Mollie snapped right into the pretext. I had no idea how far she would take it, though.

We rang the bell. A burly man in his fifties answered. We could hear the sound of a sports event on the TV in the background. From an interior room a woman's voice called, "Honey, who is it?"

"Isn't there an estate sale here today?" I said.

"No," he said. "What address do you have there?"

I showed him the scrambled numbers and he said, "That's down a few blocks. Two blocks that way." He pointed.

"Oh my gosh, silly me," I said.

"Well, good-bye," he said. "Walk in the light of God."

We already knew he was a Christian pastor and that he was very fundamentalist, so this was perfect.

"Oh, do you know any Mormon blessings?" Mollie said, knowing it would incite him. "I'm LDS."

Mollie had been a Mormon at one time in her life. Her brother was still a bishop.

"Oh, Lord help you." he said. His face changed right away.

"Well, why do you say that?" Mollie said. "Mormons are Christians."

"No, they are not Christians!" Right away he was yelling. "They're devil-worshippers."

Mollie was doing a superb job of distracting him. That gave me the opening to draw out his wife. In short order we were trading recipes and talking gardens. She told me about how they had taken their boat out for Father's Day.

Meanwhile, the conversation on the porch was spinning out of control.

He was saying crazy things about Mormons. He said that there was a special room in the Temple where they have sex and that Mormons have to wear underwear that they can never take off, even to bathe.

"Tell me," he asked Mollie, "were you married in the Mormon church?"

"Yes, I was."

"Then you know when you're married in the church, they feel your private parts during the marriage ceremony. My father-in-law was a bishop and he says they do that every time."

"Well, your father-in-law is on crack," Mollie said. "My brother's a bishop. I love my brother and I do not appreciate the things you're saying."

"Well, we love Mormons," the pastor huffed. "But we're not going to love them to hell."

"So only fundamentalist Christians go to heaven?" She asked. "No Jews? No Catholics?"

"That's right." He was gesticulating, waving his arms around. Not in the least impaired. "Mother Teresa is in hell."

This was getting way out of hand. I extricated myself from his wife and rejoined Mollie. I tried to distract her. We had to be able to visit here again.

I turned so he couldn't see my mouth. "Mollie." I got her to look at me. "Come back," I mouthed at her. "Come back, Mollie." I pinched her to make the point.

I could almost see her stepping back from the brink.

"Wow," she said. "Whew. This has been, like, interesting. Maybe my views are wrong. I'd like to learn more."

He invited her to come to church. We did go to their church the next day and it was actually quite lovely. But there was some kind of problem, so he never showed up.

Mollie called him a few weeks later. We knew he was lying, but we still needed proof. She said she was in the area and wanted to stop by. She said, "I got your number from the church directory. I have really been thinking about leaving my church and I really would like your guidance."

It happened that he and his wife were having a barbecue, and he invited Mollie to join them. She couldn't, but she did stop by in time to get some great tape of him cutting down trees and loading up debris into a wheelbarrow.

One more visit and Mollie might have dedicated her life to Christ. Too bad. We could have gotten such great footage of the pastor lifting Mollie out of the baptismal water.

Some of our insurance fraud cases were enough to make a cynic out of anyone. One time we did two fraud cases in a single day. We coordinated them because we had to drive to a town a few hours from Boise to gather evidence.

We knew the first man was a landscaper who had his own company, Garden Vistas Landscaping. We got to the site and he was already working. We were amazed, because if this guy was impaired, then I wanted to be impaired. He cleared the walkways with a blower. He trimmed hedges. He edged the yard. He dug holes and planted trees. He spread what looked like a full yard of cedar chips.

The truth was, we probably had enough tape after the first half hour, but we were fascinated. This man was a working fool. Then he got into his truck to drive away. As the truck pulled out, we caught sight of the magnetic sign on the side. Fred's Landscaping. We'd just spent two hours taping the wrong guy.

The second case took us to a bed-and-breakfast run by a charming couple. The man had been injured in a car crash that had occurred in the parking lot of a grocery store. The cars were going about ten miles per hour. He had to wear a back brace and he had tremendous difficulty moving about.

Mollie and I said we were from a women's group looking for a B and B to hold a retreat. Would they mind if we taped the grounds?

They said that we were free to tape outside, but not in the living area. We did some perfunctory taping outdoors and then we came in to say good-bye, but really to see if there was a way to document his condition.

Just as we walked in, the woman called out, "Dinner's on!"

"Oops, I forgot to turn off the camera," Mollie said, and of course she turned it on just as our subject went leaping off the couch to get his meal. We brought the tape back to the insurance company and they gave him a private screening. The word came filtering back that he was displeased with us.

Which was not very nice, after we'd made him a star, and all.

Fortunately they weren't all about trying to smoke out insurance cheats. There were people who were legitimately impaired, and in those instances we would bring our observations to the parent company and they would have to pay out.

Mollie once took a picture of a guy with crutches who was just barely moving across the floor. He had no idea that he was being taped, and he could hardly get down into a chair or up. He was definitely hurting. When we took the tape back to the company, they paid him. They were into him for quite a lot of money. We weren't hired by that particular indemnity company again, but I'm sure that was just a coincidence.

Sometimes we wanted to get that money shot so badly that we ended up putting ourselves in danger. When we had the kids along this was a non-issue, because their very presence made us cautious. But without them, there were times we probably should have been afraid and were not. Of the two of us, Mollie was more likely to go out on a limb.

I got a call from her late one Halloween night. She was laughing so hard I could barely understand her.

"Where are you?" I said. "What's that noise?"

"I'm in a Jack in the Box," she said, "in Nampa."

"What the heck. What are you doing in Nampa?" Nampa's not a good place to be alone at night. As a woman, in particular.

"I did the surveillance on the new client, Jazmine. I told you I was going to."

"I know, but I had no idea she was in Nampa."

"I chased her all the way from Boise. You can't believe what happened. It's unbelievable."

As Mollie followed her subject from Boise toward Nampa, the woman was speeding, just flying. She was, Mollie told me, doing seventy-five miles per hour in a thirty zone. Somehow, Mollie was able to stay with her. She didn't even realize where she was, she was so intent on not losing Jazmine. The chase took Mollie to a broken-down shack of a house in Southside Nampa. There was a party going on and a lot of people were very drunk.

While Mollie sat in her car, just trying to get oriented, the subject's car door opened and she stumbled out onto the lawn and fell on her face. She lay there not looking any too functional. In fact, Mollie was trying to decide whether she should begin CPR, when Jazmine moaned and rolled over. She staggered back to her feet and unsteadily negotiated the front stairs.

Mollie's problem was how to get a recording of this party. Every time she walked to a spot to try to film, the motion sensor light would go on and she would have to backtrack to her car. This happened about twenty times, Mollie said. She was annoyed, but she was laughing about it, too, because it was so ridiculous.

Finally she noticed that there was a gap of a few feet between a shed and the fence. She could just about wedge herself into it. There was a four-inch hole in the fence, at that spot, big enough to fit the camera lens.

"It was the most fun I've had in a long time," she said. "It was so great. I couldn't wait to tell everyone."

"All they had to do was look over the fence and there would have been this middle-aged blonde woman taping everything." I shook my head. "That would not have been so much fun."

While driving to Nampa alone at night was obviously a risky move, there were times when danger came at us from left field.

After an article about Hanady Investigations appeared in Boise's paper, *The Idaho Statesman*, a woman contacted Mollie, asking if we would consider working with her dear friend Tanya who had lupus and happened to be a psychic. If we were to consult with Tanya from time to time, it would give her spirits a lift.

Since lupus falls under the umbrella of autoimmune diseases that includes Mollie's illness, she was inclined to be more sympathetic than she otherwise might have been.

She promised to meet with Tanya to see if collaboration was feasible. Tanya gave Mollie a free psychic reading as a demo of her psychic powers. She told Mollie that her son would move to Seattle, get several girls pregnant there, and become completely addicted to meth. That was just one highlight in a three-hour reading. Since she was, in effect, interviewing for a job with us, I would have thought she'd want to predict that Mollie was going to win the lottery.

When she figured out that we weren't going to hire her, Tanya told Mollie that she wanted to hire us as investigators instead. The next step would be a meeting with me and so Mollie took me to Tanya's home. But did she think to give me a heads-up about the weirdness I was about to encounter?

Of course not.

She was always doing that kind of thing to me. I walked into the yard without a clue. The first little red flag was the big metal butterfly hung over the front gate. Then I saw that everything in her yard was purple, including the concrete walkway, a fountain made from truck tires, and an old Jaguar up on blocks.

Mollie lived with an artist, so that stuff didn't faze her. She didn't get it that it's not within my range of experience.

Inside, Tanya had about a dozen life-size mannequins. They were purple too. They were arranged in erotic poses. On the floor and the couch. On the kitchen table, for gosh sakes.

This soccer mom is not used to that kind of thing.

Tanya had a miniature greyhound, and the dog was just *yip yip yip yip yip* so that we couldn't even hear what she was trying to tell us.

"You're good with dogs," I said to Mollie. "Pick up the dog and pet it. I'll bet it'll be quiet." Tanya handed the beast to her and it promptly peed on her lap. Tanya handed Mollie a roll of paper towels without missing a beat of the story. I thought, *There you go, Molls. What goes around comes around.*

I was madder than heck at her for getting me into this.

Tanya told us that she thought she was in danger. She didn't know who was after her, but it could be the DEA or it could be an old girlfriend. She was afraid the old girlfriend was trying to poison her and her little dog too. Could we locate the ex?

I decided that if she was going to pay us, we could do that much.

We took some greens with berries and nuts—food she thought was poisoned—to a lab for analysis. We drove her to a free clinic for an exam and got her a blood test for toxics. We even took her dog to the vet. Every test was negative. This was not a vast surprise.

While we were helping to prove that her suspicions were groundless, we were also being sucked into her world. She told us she had gotten pregnant with a turkey-baster, which we knew was at least possible. Then she confided that the baby had been stillborn. She was able to manipulate us into feeling sympathy for her. She had us going for about two weeks and then the whole thing started to crumble.

I ran into Cara, a woman we knew was Tanya's good friend, and someone who knew her story.

"It's good that you're helping Tanya," she said. "She's got a lot going on in her life."

"Oh, I know," I said. "It's always hard for any woman to lose a baby."

"Oh wow, what has she been telling you?" Cara took a step back from me. "Tanya's never been pregnant."

"Are you sure? She couldn't have, maybe, kept it to herself?"

"Oh, no way. Not possible. Wow. I can't believe she told you that."

That was Strike One.

We drove over to get her to admit the discrepancy.

We found her in a reflective mood. She didn't know, she said, why people couldn't just be friendly after a breakup, why there had to be all this fighting and bitterness. She hadn't treated her girlfriend badly. She'd never done anything more than slap her and head-butt her.

Strike Two.

Then she admitted that when we found the old girlfriend, she was going to kill her. At that point she'd struck out, way out, with both of us. I wanted to get away fast, but I didn't want her to turn on us, so I said, "Oh, I know how you feel, but maybe you can just kneecap her or something. Well, you think about that, and in the meantime . . ."

We blasted out of there in a blur of spinning tires and spraying gravel.

It really hit us when we were down the road: Oh my gosh, she says she's going to *kill* her.

Tanya never did pay us, which was just fine. We found her ex-girlfriend's ex-husband and told him to warn her.

After that, Tanya called us repeatedly, but we always found a reason to turn down the work. After a while she stopped calling. We thought we'd seen the last of her and it was a massive relief.

After Tanya, we became even more selective in signing clients. We were only taking one in three as it was. Our results were good, because we just signed the clients we were pretty sure we could help. We tried to work with people who were more sane than insane, although we had learned that the line between the two wasn't always clear.

One time Mollie got a call from a gentleman who wanted to meet with her. He wanted to meet at an outdoor café, he said. When she asked him how she would recognize him, he said that it would be easy. He'd be the black man.

Mollie got all excited because he would be her first client of color. She called me and said, "Oh gosh, a black man in Boise. That never happens."

Mollie grew up on the East Coast, and to her, Idaho is oppressively and boringly homogeneous.

She did take our standard precautions when meeting with a new male client. She had Sherri Arey go with her and she set the meeting in a public place. She took her stun gun and her tape recorder so that she could tape the interview.

Her potential client was a soft-spoken, well-turned-out gentleman in his late sixties who introduced himself as Arthur Connelly. Arthur Connelly told Mollie that he believed he was being followed. Mollie asked how he knew he was and he replied that, well, he could see and hear the people. He knew that one of them was a man named Brady who had a partner named Billy.

Mollie said, "All right. But why are they following you?"

"I don't know," Arthur admitted. "That's why I need to hire you." He had approached another agency, but they had wanted to charge two thousand dollars.

Mollie then asked for the specifics: What did the people look like and what were they wearing? How does he know what to call them?

Arthur said, "Oh, the voices tell me."

The tape has a long pause while Mollie absorbs the point that's just been made. Her new client was schizophrenic. What should she do now?

You can hear the compassion in her voice as she tells him, "Look, I can't charge you money to follow someone who's not there. Someone who's just in your head."

"I understand that," he said, "but it would make me feel better, because that's what I've always wanted to do. I've always wanted to hire an investigator. Just because I'm mentally ill and have this problem doesn't mean I don't deserve the same consideration as anyone else."

Mollie said, "I understand what you're saying, but I'd never take two thousand dollars to follow voices." Mollie asked him to tell her the name of the agency that had tried to charge him that exorbitant fee.

He said, "I get social security, so cost isn't a problem. I have a great apartment now. I'm doing okay, I'm functioning. Sometimes I take my meds, sometimes not."

Mollie asked him if he heard the voices when he remembered to take his medication. He said that he actually didn't often take it, because he didn't like how it made him feel.

"Well, maybe you should take it," she said. "Maybe you should talk to someone about it."

She decided that she could help him this much: She could run the phone numbers when he received a call. For that we'd charge him a nominal fee. They settled on a tiny retainer.

Arthur shook her hand and walked away feeling great.

But when Mollie played me the tape, I said, "Oh boy. Now we're following invisible people for a mentally ill man. Do you feel good about
this? Is this something you want to be doing?"

Then Mollie started getting e-mails from him. After reading them,
I realized she was right. He really was a darling man, a sweet man. I
could tell he was feeling empowered. Taking action made him feel he
had control over a life circumstance he could not, in fact, master. The
little bit of work we did for him—and even more, the ongoing, respectful
communication—made him feel validated and important and special.

Even when the line between truth and fiction wasn't clear, our most
important role for many of our clients was to believe in them. We'd say,
"You're *right*, that's wrong. Tell us what to do, we're on your side." Even
that much made a big difference for so many people. We couldn't always
make it all right, but we could always listen.

Chapter 15
Lost and Found

"I JUST WANT TO KNOW IF HE SURVIVED THE WAR."

The woman's voice had the quaver of extreme old age. This potential client's phone call had caught me at an awkward moment. I had just sat down at Tia's manicure station. She was regarding the nails of my left hand, holding them up for her inspection with disapproval.

My hands are to Tia what the blank canvas is to the painter—a place to let her creativity go wild.

"You have only one life," she'd say, "so why would you do the same thing over and over again?" I put myself in her hands. She's embedded little gems on superlong nails for me. I've had nails painted in Scottish plaid. She's practiced on Jay and even done Casey's nails in sparkly pink. I wondered whether you'd call that a manicure or a pedicure. When I first saw them, they scared the heck out of me because I thought her paws were bleeding.

Today's design, Tia told me, would be a floral motif she was developing.

I walked with the phone outside, mouthing "five minutes" to her over my shoulder.

My caller was Esther, an eighty-six-year-old woman who was, it seemed, tying up the loose ends of a long life. One piece of unfinished business concerned a boy she'd dated at the start of World War II.

They'd met when she was vacationing in the town of Bath in southeastern Maine and he was a student at nearby Bowdoin College. He'd written from boot camp at Fort Devens. He'd written from the troop transport on the way to Europe. Then the letters had stopped. She wondered if he'd made it, whether he'd lived through the war.

I thought she sounded like a sweet lady. I'd already decided to waive my fee.

I visited Esther the next afternoon. I expected, I guess, whatever "sweet old lady" conjures. Side tables covered with framed photos. Crocheted afghans.

The house was a brick box, without a tree for shade or a hedge to break up the monotony of the chain-link fence. Kind of depressing, really.

Esther stepped out onto the front step to greet me. She was as unadorned as her home's exterior. She wore her straight silver hair in a "bowl cut," achieved, in my grandmother's day, by putting a bowl over the head and following the rim with the scissors. She had on culottes and a denim work-shirt, and, an odd touch, a brightly patterned chintz apron tied around her ample middle. She met me at the door with an upraised paint brush in hand. Not the kind of brush you use to paint houses, but to paint pictures.

"Welcome," she said. "Come meet the family." She gave the door a little push and it swung open to a room jammed with easels. On each easel, there was a smallish painting, about two feet square, and almost every painting was a close-up face. They looked sketchy to me, kind of unfinished, but I could see that that was her style.

Esther's home was unusual, but not off-putting. The back of the house was a giant window. More light poured in through skylights. With its paint-spattered wood floor and scattered easels, it was somehow homey. There was a pleasantly pungent odor that Esther identified as linseed and oil paint. Over that wafted the smell of baking. Peanut butter.

I said something insightful and clever, like, "You're an artist," and thought, *Duh, Valerie.*

"I am," she said, pointing me to a wooden kitchen chair. "You can sit there. Wait." She checked the seat for paint. "No, it's fine." She sat in a green wicker chair between two easels, facing me, and laid the paint brush on a piece of newspaper on the floor. "Don't let me forget where I put that. Would you like some tea? Cookie?"

"No. Thank you, though. I would like to ask a question about your work, if that's all right." She nodded. "Who are they? Are they friends and relatives?"

"They're my children," she laughed. "Well. The paintings are my children. The subjects are people who commissioned me to paint them and people whose faces interest me." I wondered if my face was interesting. It's not the kind of thing you can ask.

Esther pointed to the painting on the easel next to me. "That's my niece. That's the first painting I did here. I moved from the East Coast about a year ago. My son lives here. Now people have to come to Idaho if they want me to paint them."

"Are you famous? Should I have heard of you?"

"Other artists know me. I am an artist's artist."

"What does that mean?" I was intrigued. I liked the surprise of finding a house full of paintings.

She laughed. "If nothing else, it means I've been stubborn enough to outlast most of my generation. They drank a lot, I drank less. Maybe that made the difference. I'm a happy person. They were renowned for their discontent. Who knows? Maybe it's just the genetic luck of the draw."

Genetic luck of the draw. I could relate to that.

"Did you do all these since you moved here?" I noticed paintings stacked against walls and more displayed on a shelf that ran the length of two walls. "There are so many."

"Oh no. No, no. This is the work of many years. Decades. It's all out because I'm preparing for a major retrospective. It will show how the work developed over sixty years of painting."

I thought how amazing it must be to distill a whole life in that way. Life was messy while you were in the thick of it. Esther had the chance to clean it up and hang it on the wall. See what it all meant.

"Come with me. I want to show you something." She led me to an easel set apart from the others. I stood before a painting of a soldier. "Tell me what you see."

I hate it when people spring these little pop quizzes. Name the first five US vice-presidents. What countries border Chad? But Esther seemed less interested in hearing a right answer than in understanding what I made of this portrait.

The painting was different from the others. What made it different?

"Well. It's old-fashioned," I said. "The colors are darker, for one thing. It's more realistic, in a way. But, at the same time, it doesn't seem as real."

"Bravo," she gave me a penetrating look. "You are exactly right. This is a painting done from an old photograph. I let it be more detailed, more realistic. But because I didn't have the person in front of me, I didn't catch the feeling, the spirit, and that's why it's not real in a deeper sense.

"It's not a particularly good painting, but I'm glad that I did it. It's the man I want you to find. I didn't know I was looking for him until I painted him. Sometimes paintings tell me things I don't know I know. You know?" She smiled at me, her voice whimsical.

"What this one told me was that I have unfinished business with the subject and that's why I called you, my dear."

Fortunately, the man she was looking for had an unusual last name. He was Robert Brachinsong. When someone is Smith or Jones—lots of luck finding him. I mean, it can be done, but it's much harder.

I began with the Social Security Death Index. That's a database of death records accessible online for free through a number of genealogical Web sites. It is drawn from the United States Social Security Administration's Death Master File Extract, a massive list of eighty-three million people, each of whom had a Social Security Number and died since 1962. Our boy was not listed.

It didn't tell me if he had survived the war, however. I went to military. com Web site to see if I could find him there. No. I also checked on the National Archives Web site drawn from National Archives and Records Administration Office of Record Services and from a World War II memorial online registry. Not there either.

I started with the assumption that if he were alive, he had most likely returned to Maine. I did an online search of marriage and divorce records for Maine. They might not tell me where he was, but they would establish both his surviving the war and his living in-state. I found that he had married a Sarah Rogers in Portland in 1948. I did not find records of a divorce.

I looked for his driver's license records. I struck out. Another online data bank listed voter registrations. He was registered in Sagadahoc County, Ward 7 Precinct 1, which was the town of Bath. He had last voted in the 2000 presidential election. There was an address and phone number, but neither was current. If, like Esther, he'd moved in old age, he could be in a nursing home or living near adult children anywhere in the country.

Then I hit pay dirt with the Hunting Fishing license. In 2004, Maine had added a new category, the "Lifetime Hunting Fishing License" for people seventy and over. That's where I found him, in that data base. Robert Brachinsong turned out to be living near Bath, Maine, not very far from where he and Esther first met.

I gave Esther his address and phone number. I asked her what she was going to do with the information. Was she going to write or call him? She told me that she couldn't imagine intruding on his life and he couldn't really be a part of hers. Their lives had briefly intersected and then gone in very different directions. She was just glad to know that he'd made it through the war and that he had lived a long life.

I thought she was very sensible. She had a question and the question had been answered. It seemed a wiser course than the one taken by Courtney, who'd been unable to resist prying open the box of the past and digging through the contents, with unhappy results. Esther knew when to say when.

Months later I got an announcement of her exhibit at a museum in New York. I posted it on the fridge where I would see it and think of her.

Esther's case had been an easy one to solve. If she'd been Internet-savvy, she probably could have found her lost soldier herself.

Not every case was that simple. I don't think that any degree of skill would have been enough to find an adoptee's birth mom without Mollie's intuition. The case came to Spymoms through a personal contact at church. Melissa, a woman who ran a Boise day care center, had decided the time was right to initiate a search for her biological mother. Melissa was in her early thirties. Her adoptive mom was dead and so she no longer worried about whether the search would hurt her.

Mollie and I met with Melissa at the center. I remember we were sitting in little tiny chairs at a preschool-sized table looking over the papers Melissa had from her birth at a local hospital.

The hospital had done a sloppy job of blacking out the name of the biological mother and we were trying to reconstruct it. Melissa thought it looked like "Jones" and I thought the closest name was Jarvis, but Mollie kept saying that, No, it wasn't Jones, it wasn't Jarvis. She was sure that it was Purvis.

We went back and forth, with Melissa leaning toward Jones and Mollie completely convinced that it was Purvis. I really didn't know. Actually, so little of the name was visible that I was afraid that we were all just doing a bunch of wishful thinking. I didn't share that thought with the client, however.

Mollie kept on it and kept on it. Even when we moved along to discussing the deposit and going over the contract, she'd come back to the crossed-out name. I was becoming annoyed, because she wouldn't let it go. This was the kind of thing we would usually address later. There I was, trying to maintain a professional demeanor while I gave the clients an overview of our process, while Mollie stayed hunched over the sheet of paper, just out of it.

The first thing we did when we started to work the case that afternoon was to run the names through our databases. More to shut her up than anything, we ran the name Purvis. And of course a woman who came up under "Purvis" looked promising. Jean Purvis.

We knew that Melissa's biological mother had been in the Peace

Corps. We called around trying to locate a woman named Jean who was in the Peace Corps. And sure enough, one of these contacts said, "Oh, that sounds like a friend of mine, Jean Purvis. She was in the Peace Corps." This Jean Purvis lived in Seattle. She was an anti-nuclear activist and worked for environmental causes—and she was the right age.

Then we really started getting excited. It just felt right, but we needed to confirm that she was, in fact, our client's biological mother. Jay travels to Seattle every month for business, so we sent him to knock on Jean Purvis' door. He had instructions to check out whether she bore any resemblance to our client. We'd given him a picture of Melissa, so he could compare the two. Melissa was extremely tall, with curly hair.

Jean Purvis turned out to be tall, with a head of curly silver hair. She bore an unmistakable resemblance to the picture Jay had with him. He waited until Jean came out to take out her trash and he took a picture of her.

We gave all the information to Melissa and said, "Now think about what you want to do."

Melissa went to Seattle and met her mom. Jean was receptive—not overjoyed, but accepting. After the birth of her daughter, Jean had never been married nor had more children. She'd just continued on with her life. Jean and Melissa continued to see each other and, over time, developed a relationship.

About six months later, Melissa called me. She said, "Okay, now let's find Dad." I was thrilled to do more work for her. It had gone so well the last time.

Jean had provided us names of the two guys she'd slept with while she was in the Peace Corps. One of them had to be Melissa's father. The only thing was, both names were completely commonplace.

We searched nationwide and state by state, punching the two names into online databases to find phone numbers. I even called nonprofits where they might have worked. I must have made more than one hundred calls and even subscribed to a Peace Corps newsletter. I called people and said, "I was in Venezuela with the Peace Corps in 1973. One of my closest friends was John Smith. Do you know him?"

Nothing, nothing, nothing.

We sent out more than eighty letters to people with the same names. We did get a lot of responses, but they were all negative. We never did find a single person who fit. It was a major disappointment for Melissa and for us too.

I was on the Peace Corps mailing for years. I never could get rid of those people.

Another tough reunion case began with a call from an adoptive mom who was looking for the birth father of her son. This one looked easy. She had all sorts of information that made it possible to research the genealogy of the father. We found the man it had to be. He was a chef— same as the biological dad. We looked in the Hall of Records and the signatures matched. We found records that showed he currently lived in Hawaii.

I called him to break the happy news that he had a son, who'd been born in 1983.

He said, "I don't know. I did sleep with a bunch of girls in 1983. It could be my son. But I'm married now, I have a family. Don't call me about this anymore."

Two weeks later, he contacted me. "I need to know if this is my son," he said. "If he is, he needs to be part of my life. We'll welcome him into our family. We'll welcome his mother into our family."

I gave major credit to him——and even more to his wife. It was really exciting. We asked him to get a DNA sample and sent him a kit to swab.

The news, when it came, was a shock. They weren't a biological match after all.

I had to call him and tell him. He hung up on me. He never responded to us again, not to phone calls or e-mails.

I'd imposed a lot on his life. He'd had to tell his wife. I had convinced him to do the swabbing and it was all for nothing.

It's true that Valerie's plan and God's plan don't always coincide. Maybe some people are better not found. There could be things it might be better not to know. But it's really hard when people get their hopes up and believe in you and then you can't come through for them.

A case with a happier outcome began with a call from a gal on a hundred-foot sailboat who was about to set out from Marblehead, Massachusetts, to Palm Beach with her husband. Celeste wasn't sure she'd be in cell phone range for the next ten days, but she'd call us when they anchored in Florida. In the meantime, she wanted us to do some research for her.

Celeste's mother had told her that her dad, Rob Roberts, had died in Vietnam. The family had lived in Boise, so she asked us to check Boise cemeteries for his grave so she could visit him. Just when she was about to hang up, she said—and it seemed like a throwaway line, at the time— "I don't believe he's dead. I have no reason to say that. It's just a gut feeling."

Mollie tuned right into that, of course. I saw the look on her face and just knew this case would be A Cause, and billing wouldn't be a large component of it.

Mollie had, in a sense, lost her own dad when she was thirteen and her parents divorced. He had left her life and she was twenty-two before she heard from him again.

I also understood the deep longing for a father. My family had recently held a memorial for my Dad. It had been four years and I still missed him. I told my family the story of the rock he'd given me to cheer me up after my second diagnosis and I reread his note. He'd always loved and encouraged me, but over the last few years of his life we'd drawn much closer. Maybe sharing Hanady Investigations had been, in some small way, my gift to him.

We started investigating. We couldn't find Rob Roberts on the Social Security Death Index. We couldn't find a marker in any local cemetery.

I'm not sure why Celeste did this after she hired us, but she kept calling the local Boise sheriff, looking for any information they might have about her dad. She was sure he was alive. Did they know where he might be?

To our amazement, they didn't write her off as a nut job. She got a real response and it was that, in fact, they had heard he was alive and that he might be living somewhere on the West Coast. That's all they knew. Celeste thought that he'd be somewhere near the water, maybe making his living from it, somehow.

Then Mollie went to work in earnest. She sequestered herself in her room for two days, not even talking to her family, while she did intensive research into his background, his military record, anything that might help. She searched all our databases for his name—and there was a man of that name living in the Seattle area.

The database didn't list a home phone number, but there was a business number for a tugboat company in Puget Sound. Unfortunately, when she found the staff directory the phone tree didn't have his name.

Finally, in frustration, Mollie called the business and selected a name from the phone tree, a name that she zoned in on. When she heard a voice identify himself as Jim Frey, she took a deep breath and said, "I'm a PI in Boise and I have some news that Rob Roberts will want to hear. Some good news." But she couldn't elaborate or reveal the client.

I was not, at this point, overly hopeful. I thought that if I got a call like that, I'd assume it was a phone solicitor or the IRS, and not respond. But Mollie thought she might have a hit. She couldn't say why, but she felt we were close.

Two very long days later—long after Mollie had chewed every finger-nail down to the nub—Rob called Mollie. By fate, kismet or divine plan, Mollie had landed on the one person there with a personal connection to Rob Roberts. Jim Frey was, in fact, his best friend. She told him, "You need to sit down. Your daughter's been looking for you. Your ex told her you were dead. She remarried and gave your daughter her stepdad's name."

What had happened so many years ago, Rob said, was that he'd come home from Vietnam to find the house cleaned out and everything gone. He had looked for his family, but no one would tell him where they had gone. In despair, he'd signed on for another tour of duty.

Now he had a chance to make it right.

This reunion cemented a deep father-daughter bond. The fact that both loved boats and sailing didn't hurt. Celeste and her dad set sail on their life-altering adventure.

I couldn't help but compare these people who were so intent on find-ing parents, or parents who were searching hard for the biological chil-dren they'd relinquished, to other subjects who didn't seem nearly so interested in the children in their custody. For instance, I couldn't help but wince at the contrast with our old friend Monique, whose case was an ongoing thorn in both our sides.

Monique really just wasn't that interested in her little girl's welfare. More than once, when we did surveillance at her house late at night, we found the child wandering barefoot around the neighborhood. No one even knew she was outside. Once she went into a neighbor's house and stayed half an hour without anyone noticing she was gone. We could have nabbed her—and so could anyone else.

We left there determined to try harder. A child's life was at stake. We had to make a difference.

Chapter 16

Dangerous Girls

WE GOT A CALL FROM DANA, A LOCAL REALTOR.
Dana told us that she was being harassed by a woman named Angela. Angela was her former girlfriend, Dana said. Angela, her buddies, and Angela's new girlfriend were really making Dana's life difficult. When we asked Dana the name of Angela's current girlfriend, we went into shock. Her current squeeze was Tanya, our psychotic psychic.

It had been a year-and-a-half since we'd sprayed gravel in Tanya's driveway. I think, really, we had PTSD from our encounter with her. If we'd gone with our first gut response, we would have turned Dana's case down. We didn't because Dana had been given a really good reference by a friend of Mollie's, someone she'd known for years at church who is, herself, a very solid citizen. In the end, we decided to try to help Dana.

Dana had sold Angela and Tanya a house, a place that had been in her family for generations. She had given them a screaming deal. We knew right away what house she was talking about—I'll never get the sight of that much purple out of my head. But they hadn't made any mortgage payments after the first month. They were meth dealers. They were cooking up meth and selling it in the house she had sold them. They were trashing the place. There were brown and orange stains all over on the walls and carpets. The house had that strong chemical smell that always reminds me of cat urine.

When Dana tried to get them to stop destroying the property, they had turned on her. She lived close to the property, and it was all too easy for them to harass her by throwing bricks and other objects through her windows. They'd had people call her and threaten to kill her.

Dana asked us to keep an eye on them, and, if we could, to try to find definitive evidence of drug use that would get them in enough trouble to have the cops step in.

I looked at Mollie cross-eyed at this point.

Nothing—no massive retainer, nor any other incentive, including a fully paid vacation in Puerto Vallarta—would be enough to entice me into that house again. Or that purple yard.

Mollie took one look at me and said, "We don't have to go in. All we have to do is watch the outside. Go through their trash. I'll do it. You don't have to. Whatever."

This time, Rob, one of our Vocationers, had a psychic reading. We paid for it. It was one way for us to check out how things were going in that house without going in ourselves. He totally played along with Tanya's reading. When she told him that she saw that he had many sisters, he told her that, yes, as a matter of fact he did have six sisters. How did she know?

When she said she saw the color yellow in his childhood home, he said, incredible, she had amazing insight, because his family always had a yard full of dandelions, and that must be it.

He left the house convinced that she and her friends were completely nuts.

While we were working on this case, we wound up watching not only the one house, but the neighborhood in general. We picked different vantage points. There were enough cars parked on the street and enough traffic to mask our presence. For a few days it was quiet. I was beginning to think we were not going to see much. Then I began to see a pattern in the traffic, people coming and going at odd hours to several houses, and one house in particular.

We saw little boys on bicycles ride up to the side of a duplex and knock on the window, and then ride around to the back to pick up a bag and then ride off. We watched as one taxi company that uses vans drove up to the same few houses and picked up a lot of neatly packaged bags.

Of course, it was a drug-dealing kind of neighborhood.

Meth is a problem that's not confined to Idaho, but sometimes it seems as if we've had more than our share. Three-quarters of the men you find in Idaho prisons got there because of a problem with meth. The percentage is supposed to be even higher among incarcerated women.

The drugs flow up from Mexico and the border states along the I-5 corridor, the interstate that runs the length of the West Coast. Although most of the super labs are said to be in Mexico and, increasingly, in central California, they have also been found in rural Canyon County, southwest of Boise. We also have lots of small home labs in Boise, even with restrictions on over-the-counter sales of the cold medications used to make the drug. It's a regular cottage industry, in fact.

You don't need to be a chemist to separate the ephedrine or pseudo-ephedrine from the cold meds, to glean the red phosphorous from matchbook strips with acetone and hydrochloric acid, to heat the pure ephedrine and change the molecular structure, to add the caustic soda of drain cleaner, or to pass the heated mixture through a box filled with cat litter to absorb the gases. The process takes less than an hour, start to finish.

In Dana's neighborhood, the trash told the story—the matchbooks without covers, the piles of propane tanks, and bags of cat litter at houses where you never saw a cat.

We dug up quite a lengthy record for Angela and for Tanya. Tanya also had a warrant out for Failure to Appear. We would ultimately have enough to tie them to a woman who was just released from prison on a Distribution of Meth charge.

While we were doing all those hours of surveillance, Dana and her girlfriend were also collecting information. They had a video camera set up in their attic and they would train it on the various meth houses. A few days after we came on board, Dana's girlfriend, Lorraine, was waiting for the tape to run out so she could change it when she saw a woman walk up to a house. The tape was still rolling.

The woman knocked on the door of the house. No one answered, so she went to the side, peeked in a window. She must have seen that there were people inside, because she went back to the front door and knocked really hard.

The door opened and two men came out. She was yelling and shaking her fist at them. Then she turned and started to walk away. One of them grabbed her by her long hair and just slammed her down onto the cement. Then he dragged her into the house by her hair.

Lorraine was freaking out. She ran to a pay phone and placed an anonymous call to the police and told them what she had seen. She would not tell them about the tape, though, or offer to come forward and make a statement. Nothing we said to her changed her mind about that. She called us to come view the tape.

We were watching from her attic when the cops came. They didn't go inside the house, because they didn't have a warrant, but they made all the residents come out and they put them in handcuffs there in the street.

They got the lady who'd had her head bashed in. She made it through, but just barely.

Then they were all gone and the duplex sat empty for weeks.

Dana's problem with her house was ongoing. Mollie talked me into doing a night raid on their trash. The dumpster was easily accessible from the back alley, she pointed out, so the risk would be minimized. We had done enough surveillance by then to know that they went clubbing on Thursday nights.

That little plan ended in the wild car chase through the streets of Boise and our rescue by our boys in blue. It ended in my complete conversion to Lorraine's point of view—that these are meth dealers, so high and paranoid that they mistook us for DEA agents, and that meth messed people up.

A day or so later, I went and found Scott alone in the garage, which he'd claimed as his place to hang with friends and shoot pool. I sat him down in one of the overstuffed chairs he had out there and I said, "Whatever this sounds like to you, please just listen. Promise me, promise me on my life—on your mother's life—that you will never use meth. If you have to do something, make it pot. Cocaine, even. Just not meth."

Scott looked at me like I was crazy.

Fear of meth became a big thing for Mollie and me. We were seeing so much drug use and saw firsthand its bad effects. When my kids were younger, I used to worry about pot, but now I was way beyond that.

Tina told me her meth story. Like a lot of single women in the 1980s, she had begun to use crank under the stress of trying to work and raise kids alone. It was a way to do it all, she said. At first she found, as a lot of women did, that she did get an amazing amount of work done and she never needed to sleep. Soon, Tina and a lot of these middle-aged, middle-class women were hooked on crank.

And Tina liked it. She liked it very much. The first time she did it, she said, it was a rush like no other, and she'd spent more than a year chasing that first high, trying to catch that first rush again. Of course she couldn't, she said, because nothing's like the first time.

These days, the crank that had proved so addictive for Tina has been transformed into the far more potent crystal ice. The shards of this more potent drug gets users wired and messes with their heads.

I was beginning to think that everyone in the world was using meth. Meth played a role in almost all of our custody cases. The parent who was our subject of investigation would almost always be using meth and sometimes we'd find out that our client was also using it.

And we were with these people a lot. We were around them. When we'd pretext, we'd have to get right into their heads for the pretext to work. That means we were trying to think like them. You have to play the game, like you're their buddy. And that was creepy.

I watched the powerful effect that the substance had on people. I watched as people gave up everything for it—their looks, their children, their home, their relationship with their spouse, their family, their spiritual well-being.

In the end, their life.

I was getting cynical. I stopped thinking of everyone as "innocent until proven guilty," and started to think people were "guilty until proven innocent." I was drifting in the direction of "Guilty. Period."

It was affecting Mollie even more, because she had started out ultra-trusting. She had been this totally open, naive, wonderful person. She'd had to learn to be distrustful. I still beat her hands down in the cynicism department, though.

If a client or someone we were communicating with on a case promised to do something, Mollie still believed they'd come through. Not me. I'd say, "No they won't. They won't do it."

Unfortunately, I was right a lot of the time. Most of the time.

When I'd first started pretexting and people asked how it was I could lie when I didn't want my kids to lie, I'd say, "Oh, it's just acting. It doesn't affect my interaction with people in my life." But it had affected me. I was more likely to take more advantage of situations than I used to be. I suppose that could be taken as being less ethical. I was no longer even sure anymore.

I do know that I turned, more and more, to faith. I had been the kind of person who prayed only when times got tough or in church. Now, both Mollie and I relied on it. It was like prayer was an antidote for poison. That's not a bad metaphor, actually, because the sordid world we'd become immersed in was a kind of poisonous sea that could have drowned us without God's help.

I don't know what I would have done without that raft to cling to. Soon, I'd be tossed into the heavy seas of the toughest cases I'd ever faced, and, beyond that, the toughest challenge of my life.

I'd float on faith, praying not to go under.

Chapter 17

Battle of the Exes

"WE'RE FROM OUTREACH TO INMATES."

Mollie shifted the load of official-looking papers and clipboard from
the crook of her left arm to her right. She peeled off the top sheet, handing it through the crack of the door to the woman inside, whose name,
we had been told, was Crystal.

Crystal's soon-to-be-ex, Jim, was our client. Crystal, who was now
scanning the paper Mollie had handed her, had outstanding warrants.
She was going to serve time, and while she did, Jim—a truck driver whose
extended family had pitched in to hire an attorney—was hoping to gain
custody of the three children who were his. The fourth, the oldest, had
a different father. Our Outreach pretext was to get in the door so that
we could document how the kids were living to strengthen his case for
court.

"We help women who might become incarcerated to keep custody of
their children," Mollie said. "We've put together a gift basket for your family." I showed Crystal the basket we'd assembled. It had clothes, manda-
rin oranges, toys, organic soda. There was a gift certificate to Wal-Mart,

and one for Albertson's. It looked darn good. In fact, Mollie had become convinced that we should do baskets as a sideline.

We heard the sliding click as the chain was removed and the door opened to reveal a woman we knew a lot about, on paper. We knew she was thirty-seven, but she looked ten years older. She wore no makeup and her face was slick with sweat. As I stepped over the threshold, the August heat hit me like a mallet. From the next room came the pounding of feet on stairs and what sounded like gunfire—presumably from the TV.

"This is Mollie and I'm Valerie," I said.

"I'm Crystal," she said, flatly. She pulled a smoke from her back pocket, in one practiced motion, and lit up. She took a deep drag, incising the pucker wrinkles around her mouth one notch deeper.

I read somewhere that it takes a thousand repetitions of a grimace to start a wrinkle. Lines that deep in a young face meant she'd smoked for decades.

Crystal pointed to three kids frozen with surprise at our intrusion, plastic toys clutched in each small fist. They ranged in age from about ten to maybe three or four. "That's Brandon, Brianna and BoyBoy." The kids were all barefoot. Crystal wore a tight red tank top and blue jeans cut short so that the front pockets stuck out below the ragged edge of the material. When she turned and led us into the living room, crescent moons flashed.

As I looked around for a clear surface to sit on, the urgency of our client's desire for custody came into focus. The day we agreed to take the case, we'd said our standard start-of-the-case prayer that we be able to pass on God's love to these people.

Now, looking around, I thought maybe we should have prayed first of all for a mop and some bleach. The place was dirty. I'm not talking standard disorder or even the intense clutter of a working mom with young kids. I'm talking filth.

On the kitchen counter, a box mottled with grease stains held the congealed remains of week-old pizza. A garbage bag spilled paper plates, beer bottles and soda cans onto battered linoleum broken through to the substrate. Around the ceiling, flies held an insectoid NASCAR race.

In the living room, faded plastic toys lay scattered over carpeting buried under newspaper inserts, half-eaten cheeseburgers, fast food wrappers and unopened junk mail. It was a tidal wave of trash. At the same time, the absence of furniture gave the room a stripped-down feel. The walls were the same. There were no photos, no pictures, not even a push-pinned calendar. But handprints spanned the space between gouges, scratches and dents. The walls were both empty and full, an eloquent record of a jangled and disordered family life.

I glanced at Mollie, who just rolled her eyes.

Crystal knocked a pile of laundry from a chair.

"You wanna sit?"

We sat.

She kicked an ottoman to the wall and plopped down.

"You," she said to the kids, "get out. Go play."

The three turned and ran into the scrubby yard, slamming the screen door so it bounced on the frame.

"You have a cat," I said. It was more of a statement than a question. I hadn't seen kitty, but the shag carpeting emitted waves of eye-watering ammonia.

BoyBoy, who had slipped back into the house, sidled up to lean against his mom.

"Ugh," she said, giving him a little shove. "Get *off* me."

Dirty is one thing, mean is another.

We had to make friends with Crystal, though, so that we could visit again. Jim was sure that she was going to try to hide the children when she went to prison, so our job was to uncover her plan.

She wasn't an unknown quantity. When Jay and I were first married and I had worked for Idaho Department of Health and Welfare I had met other mothers like Crystal. It had not affected me so much then. I had been a different person.

In those days, they put the person with least seniority into Child Protection because nobody wanted it. I had no children. I didn't even like kids. I could do the job with detachment. Now, thirty years later, after raising my own children, I could never do that job again. It just kills me to see children living in bad circumstances, and all the families doing horrible things that you never even imagined could happen to people.

Child custody cases were always the cases that I got hung up on. They were the cases I had problems with. Working the cases meant coming up against the ways people hurt kids. They don't have to hit them to hurt them.

For so many parents, the children were pawns in the ongoing war between the exes. For instance, we had learned that our clients were usually thrilled when we found out that the mother of their child was a meth user. Once we had evidence of drug use, they had evidence for the court.

And I'd think, *That's his mother. Why are you so happy that the person your child has to spend a good deal of his time with is a meth user? When you think of that poor kid . . .*

Then there were the parents for whom the kid was kind of beside the point. A good example was the client we had who was a fireman. He wanted us to find evidence that his wife was cheating on him.

In the course of investigating her, we discovered that she was letting their little two-year-old play outside the apartment complex totally unsupervised. We decided to document this neglect for him. We turned on the camera and walked up to the little girl and said, "Hi, Susie. We're friends of your mom. How are you doing? You want to dance for the camera? Want to come to the car? We've got candy in the backseat."

She was nodding. She wanted to come. At that point we stopped. We had enough on film to prove how endangered that toddler was through Mom's neglect. But when we tried to play the tape for Dad, he just brushed it aside. He said, "What I want is proof that she's sleeping around. I want proof she's cheating on me."

"But you've been talking about custody too," we said. "Isn't this good for custody?"

He just wasn't interested in what was happening to his little girl.

Another case where we had to watch a child being hurt without being able to help was a particularly vicious custody fight. A lot of times in custody cases, the accusation of molestation is thrown around. But in this instance, the court psychologist had confirmed that there really was molestation and even I could see the behavioral signs of abuse.

The fact was that we had found a copy of the psychologist's report in the trash, so we had seen the evidence ourselves. The boy had been abused. The little boy's father was accusing the mom of the molestation. But the more we worked the case and the more we found out about the stepmom—the father had remarried—the more uncomfortable we both became.

We were spending a lot of time with both sides. We began to see red flags on the stepmom. She was young, but this was a third marriage. She'd lost kids from both her first and second marriages. We couldn't see any way the biological mom was anything but an excellent parent. Believe me, we gave her a close, close scrutiny. But there was an undeniable gap between the good way the real mom treated this child and the way the stepmom had with him, which just felt *off*.

It was just a creepy feeling we had, a sick feeling when we saw the stepmom with the child. It was nothing you could point to. It was nothing you could put a finger on. But first Mollie, and then I, came to believe that we were working for the wrong side. We were actually working for the molester.

All we could do was quit the case. We backed away and were left to wonder what we were supposed to do. We couldn't exactly go to the police and say, "We have this *feeling* that something's wrong here."

I called Jeff and agonized on the phone. All he could say was, "Mom, you did what you could do." Jay also did his best to comfort me.

Still, the bottom line was that we had to walk away from a suffering child.

We had another case of abuse that spanned several generations. We had been hired by Suzanne, a widow whose husband had committed suicide. He had left a suicide note pointing to the pervasive sexual abuse in the family. He just couldn't take it anymore, he wrote. His wife confirmed the story he had outlined. She wanted us to gather enough evidence to end it once and for all.

For decades, the Grandpa Molester had abused his children and grandchildren. He'd gotten away with it for all the years that the extended family had lived together in one house. Suzanne was convinced that Grandpa Molester's wife, Nana Ruth, knew all about the abuse, but she wasn't talking. She had been accused of molesting a grandson.

At last it seemed that the secret was going to come out. The cousins and grandchildren were now old enough to speak up, and had. The case would come before the court in a month.

Then a bizarre complication intervened. One of the grandchildren won the Washington State lottery. He won millions and millions of dollars. The first thing he did was start paying hush money to help Grandpa and Nana Ruth. He paid off a bunch of cousins, giving them thirty thousand dollars each to keep quiet when the case came to trial.

That was when Suzanne hired us. She said, "I want you to follow him around, see where they go. Try to find out what their plans are. See if they try to buy somebody off."

"I don't know how we can do that." I shook my head. "It's such a sensitive subject that I don't know how we'd even open a conversation about it."

Still, we decided to go ahead and try. We followed Grandpa to a new property that the lottery winner had purchased for him. By the time we parked, he was already on his tractor with his little hat on. We figured he would be there for a good while.

I said, "Let's go talk to Nana Ruth. She's by herself. She's the one who will be open, if anyone will be. He certainly won't." We headed to the old house, where the abuse had taken place.

Suzanne had told us that the house was for sale, but there was no sign out front. If it was, that would be our opening to talk to Nana Ruth. We'd tell her we were looking for property for my father. We had picked a flyer from another house down the street that was for sale so it looked like we were checking out other properties in the neighborhood too. If Grandpa Molester's house wasn't for sale, we were sunk.

We decided to take a chance. It was worth it if we could help nail these two.

Nana Ruth answered the door, wiping her hands on a dish towel. She was the most innocuous-looking grandma ever. I spent more than two hours in her presence, but I'm hard-put to describe what she looked like. I'd do better describing the dish towel. I remember gold-rimmed bifocals on a beaded chain, salt-and-pepper hair, a squarish body. Her face is a blur, though.

She absolutely was the epitome of ordinary. This woman gave the impression that she had never done anything more evil than buy spendy fabric to make a quilt. I could imagine her having lunch with her family at Denny's, I could imagine her at church. I could imagine lots of things, but it was almost impossible to imagine the woman before me molesting a child. Except that she had.

We told her why we were there—my dad wanted to buy property. We apologized for the inconvenience if the house was off the market, but we were interested if it wasn't.

"Well, you just come on in," she said. "Let me get you both something. Lemonade or iced tea? Sit while I collect myself." Mollie and I sat at the kitchen table while she fanned her face with the dish towel.

"Oh my," she said. "Oh my. Don't you just hate this heat? I want the next place to have air-conditioning."

Mollie didn't miss the opening. "So you are selling this place?"

"Oh yes. We want to. We're putting it on the market this week. It's just . . . you know what it's like to keep it clean for people to see when you're selling. And then, you have a bunch of strangers poking around. No offense."

"None taken." That's right, Nana Ruth, you wouldn't want people peering into the dark corners of this house.

She showed us around. The place was a little battered from all the people who had lived in it, but not in bad shape, really. My overall impression was that it was so ordinary. There was no physical manifestation or trace of what went on here. I realized I had wanted there to be some mark of evil on Nana Ruth or her home, something out of the ordinary to point to. I was looking for something so definitively different that I could say, "See. They are like this and I am like that. They, the evildoers, are completely different from me."

I asked if she had a flyer we could take. We were sitting, by then, with her in the living room.

"So, do you have a house in mind?" I asked her innocently.

"Our grandson bought us property to build on," she said.

"Oh my, lucky you," I said. "It's fabulous that you have such a loving grandchild that he would buy the property for you." I added, "You know, I really like this house, I'd like it for myself, except that I have grandkids. There's no room for grandkids."

She said, "Oh no, there's plenty of room for grandkids. Ours are here all the time."

"Oh, that's so great," I said. "Aren't they just the biggest blessing? I don't know what I'd do without my grandkids. And my whole family, really." Mollie nodded.

Nana Ruth was silent. I pressed on the point. "I mean . . . family. What else is it all about? And now my family life is even richer, because I have a fabulous daughter-in-law."

"Well, I don't," Nana Ruth said, flatly. "My daughter-in-law is the devil."

All right. "My gosh. That's terrible. What's she done?"

"It's unbelievable. This was the happiest family and she has literally destroyed our lives. She killed my son. She did it. I know it and she knows it and God knows it. She made his life a living hell. He'd come to me and I'd say, 'Divorce her. We'll stand by you, son.' But he'd go, 'No, Ma. She's just unhappy. How can I turn my back on her?'" Nana Ruth's eyes welled.

"Well, one day he came to me and he said, 'Ma. Whatever happens, I want you to know how much I love you and Dad.' I said, 'What do you mean "Whatever happens?" What are you afraid of, son?' He wouldn't answer me. And that was the last time I saw him alive. She poisoned him in the night."

"No. She didn't."

"Yes. As unbelievable as it sounds, she did it. When I confronted her with it, she threatened me. She told me 'I'll fix it so that no one will believe you and you will go to prison for one hundred years.' Well, she framed us for his death. She wrote a so-called suicide note that's just full of crazy, crazy stuff, things you can't imagine, and now we're the ones in trouble." She was wringing her hands. "And she's young and pretty and we're just two old people. We don't know what to do, we just don't know. Once certain things are said, people just believe them. Thank God for our friends. That's all I can say. Heaven bless our friends."

Nana Ruth pointed to a long sheet of paper on the coffee table before her.

"You see," she said. "That's a list of two hundred and twenty people who are writing us letters of support. They know what good people we are. They know how evil she is." Nana Ruth looked me squarely in the eyes. She looked at Mollie.

"I have this to say. Get on your knees and pray every morning and every night that God keeps someone so evil away from your family. If I had known, really known who and what she was, I would have gone to her and said, 'Take my money, take my house. Whatever it is that you want you take it—but leave my family alone.'"

The kicker was, I was starting to roll with the story. She had that timbre in her voice of absolute conviction, that quaver of sincerity and grief. She nearly convinced us.

We'd heard so many stories from so many people, but this woman was good. She almost had us believing that she was being victimized. We almost started having sympathy for her. We almost were ready to give her a hug. Without the statements from the grandchildren, I might have done it.

We don't know if she pulled off her act in court. Whatever the outcome, her son was dead, and nothing was going to undo that damage. Legal action could, though, stop the abuse that was being passed down the generations like an evil inheritance.

We watched as a client—a dad who'd had a stroke that left him in a wheelchair—lost custody of his two sons to a drug-using mom.

Our client lived with his parents, and they were a strong, supportive family. He was cognitively on top of things, but his disability made it hard for him to speak, to be articulate in expressing himself. We both were convinced that that difficulty played a big role in what happened. The first time he'd gone to court, he hadn't been allowed the time it would have taken to express himself. He couldn't speak for himself and no one could speak for him. This time, he was allowed to speak, for all the good it did him.

His ex had just been arrested for possession of cocaine and meth. We had found a letter that she had written from jail to meth distributors and users. In the letter, she admits that she was high when she was arrested and that she'd had drugs on her person. She spelled it out. There was no doubt.

We watched, open-mouthed, as the judge characterized the mom's drug use as "probably recreational" and gave her custody.

The last time I checked, meth and cocaine were illegal. There is no such thing as the recreational use of meth and cocaine.

It was horrifying to see that gentle soul lose his kids to that woman.

With custody cases like these on our plate, you can see why we were happy when we got a cheater case, a long-lost love, or an adoption search. We were starting to really feel the strain.

Meanwhile, our longest-running case, Grandma and Monique, rolled on. Grandma called Mollie's iPhone over and over. Grandma had "first right of refusal" when Monique left the girl—meaning that before she hired a babysitter, Grandma had to be offered the slot. But Monique ignored that and so we'd have her on contempt. Our client got emergency custody, but it never stuck. The judge threw it out of court, every time.

It was heartbreaking. Of course it was. We saw how the little girl begged her grandmother not to leave her at home. We gave Grandma's attorney proof that Monique was using coke, but even that didn't make any difference.

Then we caught her at it again and a different judge court-ordered her into treatment and gave Grandma temporary custody. Her "treatment" was outpatient at a church clinic two times a week. In a month, she had her daughter back.

Then we were in court for another case and Monique was there with her older daughter. She was paying a fine because the daughter had been picked up on a Drunk and Disorderly with traffic violations, so Mom had to pay a $175 fine. The traffic violation turned out to be driving the little girl around without a car seat. She wasn't supposed to be left in charge of the child, period, but that didn't seem to matter.

Another disturbing feature of the case was that both Mollie and I had observed that the child seemed as afraid of being left with her sixteen-year-old sister as she was of being handed over to her mom. Both of us began to think that there was a good chance that some abuse was happening at the hands of the teen sibling. Grandma had formed an attachment to the older girl when her son was married to Monique and so she didn't want to hear it.

Meanwhile the older girl was dressing Goth and skipping school. She got DUIs and still drove, following the pattern set by her mom. It sounds horrible, but she was almost a throwaway at this point. If there were someone willing to focus intense love on that kid and provide really good therapy, maybe she could survive, but where would that have come from? Without it, she was headed to become what her mother is. That's what happened to Monique's son, who was in prison.

Meanwhile the child who'd been six years old when we took the case turned nine.

We sat down with Grandma. "This is costing you a lot of money," I said, "And we're not getting anywhere."

She just said to keep working.

We continued to collect information for Grandma's attorney, although we both wondered what good it would do.

This case was woven through everything we did. Everybody worked it—all our contractors, even our Vocationers—because it was there all the time. It was just an ugly thing. I couldn't see any perfect solution, or any really good solution, or even any reasonably good solution. I swore that the only new custody cases I'd take would be ones that were specific and circumscribed.

We'd just had one like that. We investigated a dad who took the kids to a construction site and locked them in his pickup for the day while he worked. It was easy for us, because we just had to take pictures and we didn't have to decide who was right and who was wrong. It was pretty obvious. This was so much harder.

We were beginning to think that the only way to get custody for Grandma would be to catch Mom driving back and forth in front of the police station at ninety miles an hour, shooting heroin into an arm stuck out the window, while drug paraphernalia and empty whiskey bottles tumbled out of the car and the little girl bounced around in the backseat.

Maybe even that wouldn't be enough.

Finally, I called Grandma. "It's been years," I said. "Thousands and thousands of dollars. Buy her out. The only reason she's keeping the kid is for the nine hundred dollars a month in child support. Buy her out."

It was so unbelievably frustrating. I began to wonder if the tangle of conflicting needs would be sorted out so that justice would truly be served.

I was perfectly positioned to see it all, all the danger these children were in, but I was fundamentally unable to save them. On some level it made me frantic, as if I saw a toddler playing on the railroad tracks and couldn't move or cry out.

What I couldn't know, as I wrung my hands over these kids, was that I was on the tracks too—and the train was coming.

Chapter 18

The Downside of Empathy

LISTEN TO ME. YOU HAVE TO . . . YOU HAVE TO LISTEN to me."

I grabbed Jay by the shoulders and shook him, hard.

"*The kids, the kids, the kids.*"

The house was on fire. We had five minutes to grab the children and get out. Smoke roiled up between the floorboards. But I couldn't get the words out. Jay just looked at me, puzzled, and shook his head.

I was shaking, Jay was shaking me.

I was awake and the TV was blaring. I had fallen asleep to *Survivor* again. No, it was the alarm. Dang, I'd slept through the alarm. I jumped out of bed, pulled some clothes off the hangers and got dressed.

That dream stuck with me all the way to court. Jim and Crystal's custody case finally came to family court. I had to testify.

I knew the house had state-of-the-art smoke alarms. The kids were now old enough to have their own kids. But I couldn't shake the oppressive feeling. A lot of my dreams these days were about trying to get someone's attention in an emergency. Getting them to listen to me. Often I could wake to the dream and lie there trying to figure out how I could fix the dilemma. It kept going through my head—if I'd said that, then the person would have said *that*. If we'd done this, then we wouldn't have this problem.

It never seemed to help.

We had visited Crystal of the trashed apartment and neglected kids several times over the course of the surveillance. We had brought smokes for her and clothes for the children. We'd stocked the fridge with soda and groceries. It made us feel a tiny bit better to know that we were able to do that much for those kids. They'd eat well for a little while, however things turned out.

The children soon figured out we always came bearing gifts. We'd ring the doorbell, and by the time their mom answered the door, they would have formed a little line—quiet, polite, hopeful.

For Crystal, we were an audience, and she liked it like that. She had a lot of things to get off her chest. When I think about her, today, what comes to mind is not the apartment or even those poor kids, but Crystal—shoehorned into clothes two sizes too small, parts of her always on the brink of spilling over or falling out.

I was waiting in the hallway for my turn to testify. Mollie was inside the courtroom with our current Vocationer, when Crystal made her dramatic late entrance—clad in a tight business suit without benefit of blouse or bra. She hadn't gotten more than halfway down the aisle before the judge ordered her arrest for outstanding warrants. She was handcuffed and carted away.

She had told us she had a plan to go to jail when it suited her schedule, but since she hadn't shared her plan with law enforcement, never mind getting their approval, the warrants were still in force when she arrived at court.

They called me to testify. They wanted me to be the one to testify, rather than Mollie. When it came to these custody cases, her conviction sometimes got the better of her professional detachment. I was regarded as the cooler head.

But I was ready to be outspoken when it came to describing how it was for these kids—their clothing, their nutrition, their medical care, the general level of maternal concern. Bring it on.

I was waiting in the hallway for my turn to testify. I wasn't doing the usual routine of mentally rehearsing what I was going to say. Instead, I was chewing over what I'd just heard, which was that Crystal had managed to slip past us and hide those children. Of course we can't do twenty-four-hour surveillance, but I was still kicking myself for not stopping her.

I had no sooner started speaking then Crystal's mother and sister began putting their hands up and waving at the judge and in every way trying to get his attention. When they didn't get official judicial notice, they made do with muttering—and none too quietly—their opinion of my testimony.

I got through it without letting them rattle me.

The court awarded custody to Jim.

Then, at last, the judge asked for the relatives' input. Unfortunately, from their point of view, he only wanted to hear one thing from them. He wanted to know where Crystal had hidden the children. They refused to tell, and so they were also cuffed and hauled off to jail.

Mollie, Sandy and I took off like a shot from there. We went to a Starbucks and treated ourselves to white chocolate double mochas. I was just licking the foam off the stirrer when Mollie's iPhone chirped.

"Don't answer it," I said, knowing that of course she would answer it and of course we would do whatever they asked us to.

Jim and his attorney were on together, Mollie said, and they wanted us to look for the children.

"I have to leave early tomorrow," Jim told her. It was already late afternoon. "I have to get home and go back to work. Please, please help me find my kids."

The attorney confirmed that the best thing we could do was to find the children at once. He e-mailed us a huge list of addresses. Not only did Crystal have a giant family, they were scattered throughout Boise and outlying areas. Any one of Crystal's relatives might have hidden the children. These were people living under the radar. They didn't cooperate with outsiders.

Mollie and I took the list, but we stopped to get gas and more coffee before we set out. We also could not set off to do this thing without getting spiritually centered. We held hands across the table and prayed:

"If it is Your will that we find these children, then help us to do it in the best way we can, doing good and not harming anyone. If it isn't, lead us to help and comfort Jim."

Mollie called Bill and asked him to pick up the kids. I called Jay to let him know that I would be late and to make sure that Casey had dog food.

It was going to be a long, long night.

We began knocking on doors. Before we set off, we'd organized our-selves to make some geographic sense of the long list. We stuck to the plan, driving from neighborhood to neighborhood, becoming more and more grim as we got doors slammed in our faces. We took turns doing the actual knocking, because that way one person didn't have to catch all the negativity.

Our little Vocationer couldn't believe it. She kept asking us, "Is this what the job is like? Is it really this bad all the time?"

Bad? We were counting ourselves lucky that no one had come to the door with a loaded shotgun.

We were carrying stun guns, but still. This kind of thing brings out the passion in people. I understood that intensity. While I had seen enough to know that life with our candidate for Mother of the Year would leave these kids irreparably damaged, and therefore we needed to find them, there were people who were going to be collateral damage when we did—chief among them the brother who would be left alone with that mother.

In any case, we weren't having any luck. We were working our way down the list. I didn't have a feeling that anyone we'd talked to knew more than they said.

It was almost midnight and still we hadn't found anything. We had made a loop from downtown Boise that included Garden City, Caldwell and Nampa. Now, headed back to Boise, we had to ask ourselves whether the time had come to give it up. We decided to do one more house. This house belonged to one of the great-aunts. It looked well-kept and had a nice little garden. In the garden, a tricycle was turned over on its side.

We parked a few blocks past the house and walked back. As we stood outside the fence, Mollie saw an upstairs curtain pulled open. A small face looked down on us.

We called the attorney and he told us what to do: Go get the kids.

I quickly volunteered to notify Jim and the police, and to wait outside for them. It killed me to do it. When it came down to it, we were separating children from their older half-brother. It was possible that he would not see them again or not for years. Also, I had some compassion for the great-aunt. She had not done the things that sent Crystal to jail. She was losing these kids too.

We could have left. Our PI job was done when we notified the attorney and Jim where the kids were. But we didn't want to the police to go in after them. We thought it would be kinder to do it ourselves. We didn't want it to be ugly for the children.

Mollie and the Vocationer started dressing the children, getting them ready to leave. The police arrived and knocked on the door to check that things were all right. I hid behind them. I couldn't step inside.

Jim arrived. He was grateful. The police walked the children to him. The great-aunt and the little boy were framed in the doorway. He was bewildered, saying good-bye to his siblings, but he had no idea why or what it meant. The great-aunt did. She collapsed onto Mollie. Mollie told her over and over, "It's not your fault. You didn't do it, you didn't make this happen. Crystal made choices that made this happen."

The children were packed into Jim's car. I thought about how it would have been for Jeff and Scott to be ripped away from Christine. From me. I thought about how it would have been to lose Jan and Henry when we were kids together. Maybe never to see them again. Crystal and her mother and sister did not even get to say good-bye, because they were in jail. Did any mother—even one like Crystal—deserve that?

There had been times when being a woman PI had been an advantage. This was not one of them.

As we drove off, the Vocationer said, "I'm flying home tomorrow. I've decided I don't want to be a PI." She would be one of the very few Vocationers who didn't stay in touch with us. Who can blame her? The case had me wondering if even I wanted to be a PI.

This one was positively sunny compared to the next case though.

Chapter 19
Murder or Suicide

IT WAS JANUARY 10, 2007. I REMEMBER THE DATE because I'd just passed my six-month checkup with flying colors. The few days of waiting for those test results was the only time I felt nervous about cancer. Otherwise I was a poster child for survivorship. Four years and counting.

It was a few days after getting those cancer test results that Mollie and I opened an e-mail from a distraught mom. I'd heard from plenty of upset parents, but this was different.

I read: Can you help a mother? My son died a year ago last week. His death has never been cleared up.

Shannon lived in Mountain Home, a sagebrush desert an hour from Boise. Shannon had seen us on television and decided to call. Her son, Cody, had died from a gunshot wound. The death had been ruled a suicide, but there hadn't been an autopsy. No toxicology screening had been done. Police hadn't secured the scene. A suicide note had either been posted after his death or had been overlooked by police at the scene.

There were other discrepancies and suspicious circumstances that suggested he might have been murdered. His eyes had been blackened, suggesting a fight. According to the police report he had been shot point-blank by a .38, but the bullet had not exited his head.

Law enforcement hadn't treated this family well. They wouldn't talk to them at all. The family members were haunted by the unanswered questions. They had to know what really happened.

"No," I told Mollie, "This is not our kind of thing. We're not crime scene investigators. We're not CSI."

Mollie said, "We can do this." She thought that we could apply our skills to answering the questions the family still had. We could at least gather information. The fact that we had never done a case like this made it that much more compelling. Mollie thought we would learn a lot and we would grow in the process.

The family wanted it so very badly. And I was aware that this was the first time that Mollie had pointed us in a new direction that really pushed the envelope. She had stepped up to take the lead, really for the first time. I decided that anything we found out would be helpful.

We went to Mountain Home and met with the family. Shannon, her sister, and a brother attended that first meeting. I liked them. They were plain-spoken, nice people. Unpretentious. Shannon had dark circles under her eyes. She was rail thin. A year of that kind of grief—losing your child, the worst kind of grief—leaves an indelible mark.

They walked us through the basic outline of the case. Cody had lived in an apartment above the convenience store where he was manager. It was quite a responsible job. The family was proud of him.

Cody had a girlfriend, Nicole. Nicole wasn't working at the time, and the two habitually stayed up late. It wasn't unusual for Cody to start work at 10:00 AM or 11:00 AM, so when he didn't show up for work first thing that morning, no one in the store thought much about it. They opened up without him.

Nicole had not stayed with Cody that night. However, the next morning she had gotten up early, around 6:30 AM. She had told her mother, "I feel something terrible has happened to Cody and we need to find out."

They called the store and had an employee knock on his apartment door, but there was no answer. The employees weren't worried, because they thought he just didn't want to come to the door so early.

Nicole and her mother were not reassured. They waited until nine and then they drove to the store. They sat in the car out front, mother and daughter together. Maybe they still hoped that he would stick his head out the window and laugh at them for being worried. Maybe they were delaying the moment when fear becomes fact. Finally Nicole's mom said, "I'm going to go up and open that door. You stay in the car."

I took the list of questions the family had compiled for us to answer. I scanned the bulleted points. "What if we investigate and there are still questions?" Shannon's brother said, "We don't care. It's better than what we have now." The others agreed.

We told the family we were going to treat the death as a murder and see if we could prove otherwise.

As we headed to Mollie's car after this initial meeting, Mollie said, "Val, Shannon's a tweaker." Mollie's suspicions were strengthened when we later visited the mother of Cody's former fiancée in prison. She was serving a term for meth and she accused Shannon of using the drug.

Our gut reaction was that these were good people under extreme duress. Shannon had just lost her son. Whatever she was doing was probably excusable. We decided to leave it alone, unless her drug use directly affected the case.

Our first step was to try to get hold of all the evidence we could. The police had custody of quite a few items, and we needed notes, photos— anything that pertained to the case. They would not, however, shake loose any of the evidence. We had better luck with the coroner's office. They did turn over the many photographs taken at the scene.

Both Mollie and I had sons Cody's age. It was going to be unbelievably difficult to view those images. It would be hard for anyone, but perhaps more for us, as mothers, because we understood, in the very deepest way, Shannon's grief for her child. Just the thought of a young man dying was enough to make me frozen with pure fear for my own sons. Never mind having to look at photographs of the body.

Mollie took them and went through them first, on her own. But when she handed me back the thick manila envelope, I found I couldn't open it. I put them on the passenger seat of my car and I took them home with me.

"Jay," I said. "I need your help. I can't make myself look at these pictures of that dead kid." We both sat down at the kitchen table. I said, "Preview them for me. Pick out the ones you think I can bear."

He opened the envelope. I looked somewhere else. I really don't know how long it took. I know it got dark in the course of his looking at them, because I got up and flipped on the light.

Finally he said, "All right." He had two stacks of photos in front of him. One was much bigger than the other. He slid the bigger pile back into the folder. He left the smaller one out on the table.

He got up and walked out of the room. He paused in the doorway and said, "Don't ever ask me to do that again."

I reached for the pile of pictures. I slid them across the table, slowly and deliberately. I made myself look down.

Cody was lying on the floor, in front of the TV, as if he were watching it. He had his underwear on and was covered with a light blanket. The cell phone was lying right next to him. He held the gun lightly in his hand, his fingers barely on it.

He was still good-looking, this eighteen-year-old kid with the hole in his head, but his short, dark hair could not conceal the imprint the barrel of the gun made on the side of his forehead. The entry wound was small and dark. His eyes were swollen and dark. He was smiling, a sweet, almost angelic smile.

Mollie and I re-enacted the death over and over, trying to see if he could have shot himself. After making Jay sort the photos, I wound up having to look through them all, anyway. In fact, I looked at them a lot as we analyzed Cody's death. Given the angle of the gunshot, was it feasible that he had trained the gun on himself?

I asked the police if they would release the gun to Cody's family. The case was concluded, as far as they were concerned. Couldn't they reclaim the gun?

The police also had a surveillance tape that would have showed anyone coming from or going into Scott's apartment. They also refused to release this, either to me or to the store owner. They said there was nothing useful on it, so what would be the point? The point, I said, was that it belonged to someone. Couldn't they have it back?

There was no response to that one, either. I was actually surprised by the attitude of the cops. We had not assumed that they'd done anything wrong. Why were they so afraid of releasing this information?

The coroner's office refused to talk to us, so I showed the photos to people expert in the use of firearms. I'd ask, "Does this look like anything besides suicide? Is there anything odd that raises red flags?" On my own, I began to compare these photographs to images of other suicides.

I went from person to person, trying to interest police or a pathologist in the case. Idaho has forty-four counties. I spoke to the county coroner in every one. I asked for help, but no one would have anything to do with the case. We were getting nowhere.

We interviewed Nicole's mom, who had found Cody's body. We talked to his ex-girlfriend.

It was four months of the most grueling work. Three trips to Mountain Home. We sat with this case and held on to it. It invaded my dreams and all parts of my waking life. My waking life was most of my life because I wasn't sleeping. I got a cold that lingered for weeks and turned bronchial.

The case was everything.

I kept asking Mollie, "Why did we take this on? Why did we do this?"

The police report had mentioned a suicide note posted on the door, but Nicole's mom had not seen a note. It turned out it had been posted on his back door, where police had entered, while Nicole's mom had come in the side door. We had come to believe that it wasn't a suicide note at all. We had concluded the note had been written hours before and he had posted it there because that's what he often did. He was inviting Nicole to come in, in case she came by: "If you're reading this it means you're here. Come in. I've saved a place for you." She had said she wasn't coming over, but he still held out hope that she would. That's what the note was about, we decided. But Cody and Nicole had spoken after that.

We learned that Cody's best friend's car had been parked by the apartment that night. The maintenance man said he'd had to back around the car in order to get out.

That was probably the most suspicious circumstance of all. We could not resolve that one until—after a lot of persistence on our part—the police released the tape of their interrogation of this person. When we viewed the tape, we saw that they had come down hard on him. They'd been really tough. They had asked every question we could have possibly thought to ask. We had to conclude, as they did, that even if he had been there, he didn't do it.

Then we finally got the help we needed to figure out the rest.

I got the bright idea of calling a criminology professor at Boise State. He was in touch with Idaho's forensic coroner—the most sophisticated and knowledgeable coroner statewide. If Cody had had an autopsy, this would have been the man to perform it. After all the slammed doors, it was great to have a conversation with someone who was willing to talk and was kind about it, to boot.

He had me e-mail him everything—all the photos and the questions. He promised to go through it all and get back to us.

Our forensic pathologist was as good as his word. He went through every bit of information and wrote an exhaustive report. He went over the report with us, point by point. He was wonderfully kind and really took the time to explain it all to us.

No autopsy had been done because Elmore County, where Mountain Home is located, is so small that they don't have the resources to do more than a few autopsies a year. They'd decided that this case was a suicide and so no autopsy had been performed. The black eyes were the result of being shot in the head. It was often the case that a head wound blackened eyes. The angle was consistent with a self-inflicted wound and even the lack of an exit wound wasn't out of line with suicide. Cody's family had thought that people's mouths open when they die, but the photographs showed him smiling. Our pathologist said that mouths do not necessarily open.

Nothing he'd seen pointed to murder, he said. While the police could have done a better job of explaining their conclusions to the family, they had, he said, arrived at the right answer. Our forensic pathologist was certain that the wound was self-inflicted, whether Cody had meant to do it or not.

We wanted to know about the circumstances that had driven him to the point of such despair where he'd contemplate the notion of taking his life. For one thing, we wondered why Cody's girlfriend had gotten up early that one morning, when she never usually did, and had been so concerned about him. What had happened to make her afraid for him?

Mollie shed light on this when she thought to do what the police had not. She retrieved Cody's cell phone from Nicole. She downloaded and transcribed the text messages, looking for the answer.

The phone's text messages were a record of his last communications with her. They were talking about buying a house together. That morning he'd sent away for a credit report. They were both young. The course of true love was predictably bumpy. She thought he was cheating. He'd asked her to come over and she'd said no.

In the five pages of text messages, you could see the tension building. You could see this young man getting more and more upset—so upset that he might toy with taking his own life impulsively, not really thinking that he was going to die. He didn't believe he was going to die any more than I did.

He could have put a gun to his head and said, "I'm going to shoot myself." And she could have said, "Well, you go right ahead and shoot yourself."

Once he cocked the gun and put it to his head, what would it take to shoot himself, really? Not much. You could do it without fully intending to pull that trigger.

We believed that was what happened. That was why Nicole woke up so frightened. In the cold light of day, she realized he might actually have done it.

We set a meeting with the family. We'd been e-mailing back and forth all along, so they already knew what we were going to say. I think everyone already had concluded that Cody had committed suicide. We gave them a summary of our report.

We still had one more appointment scheduled with the local coroner, the original coroner on the case. The family said that we didn't need to keep it. We had answered the questions that they had wanted addressed.

We kept the appointment because we believed that this man and the police both owed the family an apology. At least, the police did. While they hadn't done anything overtly wrong that compromised the case, they could have done a few things better. They could have released information to me. They could have treated the family with respect. We were intent on making the point. One family member, the aunt, came with us.

The coroner was very scared and defensive, at first. The first words out of his mouth were, "I don't think we did anything wrong."

By the time we left, after we'd talked about the family and he'd seen all the material, he admitted the police owed the family an apology. "I'll go talk to the police," he said. "What's done is done, but maybe next time it won't happen this way."

We helped that family in another way—or, Mollie did.

One day we were all sitting around with the family and Liz, one of Shannon's friends. They were laughing and telling stories about Cody. Mollie, apropos of nothing, said to Shannon, "Why would someone say that you're a meth user?"

I immediately felt the terrific headache coming on that I get whenever Mollie does something like this without forewarning. We had agreed not to bring up Shannon's addiction.

Shannon just laughed and said, "Because I am."

Liz, who had been busted for meth and gotten clean, said, "I never knew, all this time. I could have helped you, supported you."

Even Shannon's own daughter hadn't known. Her mom had told her she was going to quit smoking. She just hadn't said what it was she was smoking.

Shannon said, "I'm clean. I haven't had anything for two weeks."

Her drug use did help explain the way the police had discounted this family. They had noted the drug use and decided they were trash. Now, because Mollie had stepped up and said something, Shannon's move to stop using would be supported.

The County people apologized to the family. They said, "Whatever we can do to help, tell us and we will do it."

That apology helped the family find closure.

We may have helped them move toward closure in one more way.

As the case had unrolled, we had found we were spending most of our time with Cody's mother, his aunt, and the people who owned the convenience store. All these people loved Cody and didn't believe there was any way in the world he could have killed himself. The person they revealed to us was an amazing young man. We spent most of our time laughing and telling stories about him. We'd be in the back of the store, just laughing and laughing.

Usually no one wants to talk to family and friends about someone who has died. But because we wanted to know Cody, we became a place for them all to remember him. We became very close to these people. I visited Cody's grave and saw all the balloons, funny quotes, and memorabilia from all the people he had touched in his short life.

Later, Mollie got an e-mail from the family. They wrote that they were at peace.

But I was not at peace. The case had exacted a tremendous toll. I would never let myself get close to clients again, I told myself. I would not work that kind of case again. I made Mollie swear she would get rid of Grandma and Monique. Our efforts weren't doing a whole lot of good and it was just killing Mollie to be out on surveillance every night.

Maybe if we did things differently, things could be like the old days again. We would only take the cases that made us laugh, cases that saw us outsmarting the riff-raff. Every once in a while we'd go line dancing and afterward we'd go to Carl Jr.'s for a Coke.

I still had the photos of Cody on my computer. When I looked at them, I saw my son lying there and I couldn't shake the image. I went to each of my kids and said, "Promise me that nothing will ever happen to you."

I couldn't shake the bronchitis, either. I coughed and coughed.

Then I coughed so hard I cracked a rib.

Chapter 20

Pretext for Your Life

THE RIB HURT. IN FACT, MY WHOLE BACK HURT.
Mollie was on me about it. She said, "That's not right. Your ribs shouldn't be that fragile."

I went in for my May ultrasound. As usual, they wanted me to have a mammogram first. That was the policy. Never mind that there was nothing left to squash in the squisher. I told them, but they had to figure it out for themselves, every time. They wound up bringing the supervisor in and then she approved the ultrasound. It was quite annoying. That's what I was thinking about. I was not thinking about cancer.

Even when the ultrasound showed a small lump in the chest area where breast tissue would be if I had breast tissue, I was not alarmed. The technicians didn't think it was anything.

After all, I had no breasts. No breasts equals no breast cancer.

I had done everything I could to minimize the risk. I'd had a double mastectomy, I'd had a hysterectomy. I always asked, "Where does it go next? What should I be looking for?" The fact was, nobody really knew.

There was not much research on this small group, the five percent of us who had this one gene.

When my radiologist heard about the lump, he called me in. The lump had a blood supply, he said, so it should be analyzed. He sent me back to the ultrasound people for a needle biopsy. By the time I got to the clinic, I was starting to get scared. They had switched gears into an ultrakindness that was, in itself, unnerving—the nurse patting me on the arm and going, "Yes, dear, you just go in there and change." Poor dear.

My God, I thought. It's got to be something really horrible.

I just had an awful feeling about it. A bad feeling.

I said to them, "You know what? Why don't I just sit here until you can get hold of my doctor and give him the results."

They didn't like that at all. Their procedure was that you left and they sent results to your doctor, who gave you the news days later.

But the truth was, the ultrasound radiologist knew what was up with me right then and there. I could tell.

"You know, I just don't feel like going home," I said. "I'm really upset. Can I just sit here in your waiting room until you get it figured out?"

They told me it wasn't a good idea because it might not be until tonight.

But I had an answer ready: "I brought a book. I'll just read. If I get tired, I'll just lie down right there."

I knew that would make it really uncomfortable for them.

Less than an hour later they brought me the phone.

My doctor told me that, yes, it was cancer. He wanted me to get a few CAT scans. Then he wanted to remove it surgically and we would worry about radiation later. It sounded reassuringly like another verse of the same old song.

Oh well, here we go again.

This time, though, they gave me every test—MRIs, PET scans, the whole works. Then my radiologist called me into his office. I'd rather have them tell me over the phone. When the nurse says to come into the office, you know that's bad.

Jay, Jan, Christine, and my mom went with me to the radiologist's office. The doctor walked in and sat down behind his big desk. He put on a pair of glasses. He shuffled a few papers. He cleared his throat.

I said, "Well. What is it?"

He met my gaze. Anyone who thinks that doctors don't care should have been looking into this man's eyes at this moment.

"It's not good."

"How bad?"

"It's very bad."

By then I was thinking, *Give me a break here. Throw me something. How bad, what bad?*

He placed on the desk in front of me a composite of my CAT scan and MRI. On the composite, cancer showed up as hot spots. I was lit up all over.

All bones, all over.

It was horrifying, but it was not the worst, he said.

The liver was the really bad news. There were lesions. They were small, but there were a lot of them. I didn't have cancer in my brain and one other place. Kidneys, I think.

This doctor made it sound like I should go right over to the hospital and check on in. They would send someone around to administer last rites.

I put my head down on the table.

People were asking questions about liver transplants and other things. I felt like I was underwater. They were all bobbing above me on the surface and I was sunk.

I know we prayed in that office, all of us together.

The next few days were a little blurry. There were people at the house, people crying. I know I called Mollie in a panicky state. She got me through a few very tough nights. Then I went to my oncologist. Again, I brought the whole troop.

I wanted her to tell me exactly how it would go. I kept asking her, Do I have eleven months and seven days? Do I have three years and nine months?

She said, "I don't know. I'm not God. But I feel very positive because you've always responded well to treatment. We can give you the most powerful drugs and you'll probably be able to tolerate them." She was quite upbeat. I had a kind of tumor she could treat.

She wanted to start me on Herceptin, a new drug that would target my fast-growing, aggressive kind of tumor by blocking cell reproduction. I would be her first patient to receive this particular drug. I would also take a bone-building drug with an anti-cancer effect. I knew that it was unlikely that all the cancer cells would be eradicated. Hopefully, the advance of the disease would be slowed. She told me about patients who had lived four and five years after this diagnosis.

A few days later, I went to see her by myself. I said, "Let's start with the worst things first. When I do die, you are responsible for making sure I don't die in pain. Or if it's possible to come back and to haunt you, I will, and I'll poison your children, so you'd better make sure."

Good thing she'd had eight years to learn to appreciate my twisted humor. She was my dear friend and a fan of Hanady Investigations.

She said, "Sure, I get it. I promise you that part of it."

I felt such overwhelming relief.

Once the rib healed, I continued to be completely pain-free. I'd always been incredibly fortunate in this. I was back under the care of the infusion nurses and they always made me feel safe. My tumor markers were down. That was encouraging.

As usual, I found waiting for the test results the hardest part. I used every pretexting skill I had at my command to shake loose those test results. I could be the needy, helpless old lady if that got me the results. I could be everybody's favorite patient if I thought that would inspire the medical team on my behalf.

Medical personnel would be charmed because they'd seen me on TV or read about me in a magazine or newspaper. They would say things like, "Isn't that cute, she's done so much with her life. She's such an inspiration to the other cancer patients."

I was worried. I was scared. At that point I didn't care what anyone thought of me, but I did want that doctor to be on my side. I wanted that doctor to take my phone calls when I called. I made friends with the nurse, so she would be sure to help me out.

I made it my business to make a relationship with her. Her name was Beatrice and she was a single mom. Her kids were Callie and Candace, twins, but not identical twins, so it seemed all right to dress them somewhat alike, although she wondered about the long-term effects. I knew that Callie liked her hot dogs so well-cooked they were black and that Candace was afraid of dogs. I kept track of every detail, and when it came to the twins' sixth birthday, I created something I called Birthday-in-a-Bag, with party hats, favors, balloons and gifts—everything you'd need.

It's not like I wasn't sincerely interested. I was. But I also wanted something from Beatrice. I wanted her to find me memorable. I wanted her to be my ally. I wanted, at 4:00 PM on Friday, to be able call her and say, "Bea, I know it's a lot to ask. Here it is, almost your weekend. And you're headed to the lake with the girls and you've got so much to do. But could you, you know, just call that lab for me, because you know how I am, I'll worry."

Having an ally in that office made the whole thing a little more bearable.

When the Herceptin failed, which it did after a few months, I was prescribed a new regimen of pills that had to be taken in complex and varied combinations. Both my oncologist and her nurse were out of town when the medications arrived by mail.

There were twenty different pills I had to take every day—four here, two there, some with food, some without. There was one drug in two different strengths that I had to mix in certain combinations.

I used my investigative skills to contact someone who could help me figure out how to calculate the dosages and I used the Favorite Patient pretext to charm them into helping me.

In fact, I summoned all the skills I had spent years acquiring as a private investigator. Everything I'd learned was helpful now. I knew there were places you could go to, people you could look for, resources that could help—if you knew how to take advantage of them. If you had the courage to seek them out.

After I was diagnosed the first time, I had done a lot of research, mostly looking at alternative therapies. The second time I hadn't, because

I was pretty sure that I knew everything in the world about cancer. This time, I did research metastatic breast cancer.

I could, I decided, hit the ground running with breast cancer, even if it had spread. I just needed to keep track of the metastases to bone, liver and lungs.

They put me on Tykerb and Xeloda. Over time, there were other drugs, many new to this hospital. There was even a seminar for the nurses when I got on Ixempra. They were quite excited about it.

The relentlessness of a drug regimen that went on for eighteen months, with new drugs all the time, wasn't easy. At least we did not go broke, because we had great benefits through Jay's employer, Do It Best Hardware. As we went from one cutting-edge treatment to the next, I was increasingly grateful for that coverage.

I did some Spymom work, but really I was focused more on family for this time. Christine and Ben, after dating five years and being engaged for one, were to be married in January. They were planning a big-deal wedding. They had offered to pay for most of it, but we were all involved in the planning. I didn't foresee that my PI skills would contribute to the wedding, but, as it turned out, they did.

I was focusing on looking good for the ceremony. No matter what is going on in this woman's life, getting dressed up makes me feel better. I found it very heartening to note that I really did look quite good, amazingly enough. The only problem was that the chemo made my eyelashes fall out. I decided to compensate with eyeliner, and I spent a lot of time experimenting with various shades and shapes.

I was not the only experimenter. Tia was gearing up for the wedding pedicure push, so there were days when every one of my toenails was a different shade. She practiced pedicures on Jay. Only Jeff drew the line—no polish, not even clear.

I was just getting ready to think about my dress when Christine saw one that she thought I'd like, so she bought it. She was right. It was a very cute dress.

It had a weird belt with rhinestones for the buckle, so I decided to ditch the belt and have the skirt ruched. The pleats would give the dress more character than a belt, anyway. Someone gave me the name of a seamstress and I took the dress to her office. I was impressed by her, a really gorgeous, put-together lady.

You don't want your dressmaker looking tacky, right?

I modeled the outfit for her and she pinned it.

She said, "Super. Call you in a couple of days. We'll have it done."

So she didn't call, I called her. She didn't respond. A month went by. The wedding was creeping closer. I tried phoning her office number. No response.

I did a little research and found that she was associated with a particular fabric store. I went there and they were really distressed to hear that I couldn't get my dress back from her. They promised to contact her. It turned out that she'd had some kind of breakdown, they said. They hadn't spoken with her, but left a message with her significant other.

She called me, at last, and said, "Oh, we must have had our wires crossed. But I've been working on it. Why don't you come on in and we'll see if it's fitting right."

So I did, but she never showed.

Then nothing, nothing, nothing. Same as before.

I went back to the fabric store. By now, I was mad. The wedding was just weeks away.

"We'll see what we can do," they said. "We understand it's really serious."

I thought, *Sure.*

I used my PI skills to find out who owned the building her office was in. I called the property management company and said, "She's holding my dress hostage. I want it out of there. Or do I take you guys to court? Tell me what I have to do."

The property manager said, "We can't let you into somebody's office. We make a commitment not to."

I said, "Okay, that's fine. Would you let the police in?"

"Well, I don't know. What do you mean?"

"If I get a police officer to come with me to document what I'm taking is mine and he signs off and does a police report and everything, would that be enough to get my dress out?"

He told me to hold off on the police. He'd get the dress out for me.

But I waited and still nothing happened.

Finally, in a fit of frenzy, I called the fabric shop and said, "Today. Seriously. If I don't hear from her today, I have her home address and phone number. I know who her significant other is. I know who her children are. I'm going to knock on doors until I find someone who will let me into that office. And no one's going to be happy about it."

So that got her to call me back. I was, as it happened, having coffee with Jan, who already knew the whole story. My seamstress said, "Oh, I guess we got our wires crossed again. You can come and be fitted later today."

I looked at Repo Gal Jan and she looked at me. We both grabbed our purses and ran for the car.

She greeted me as if I were the elusive party and she'd been the one waiting.

"Good, you're here," she said. "Go into the dressing room and try it on. We'll see what else needs doing."

I said, "Looks perfect to me." I had not so much as glanced at the thing. "What do I owe you?"

I expected her to say, "Nothing, because I'm a maniac and I stole your dress." Instead she asked me for forty dollars.

"Can you take a credit card?" I already knew she couldn't.

I told her I'd mail it to her. "If you don't hear from me, give me a call," I said, "because there's a wedding going on and I might forget." I never paid her.

Thankfully, she'd done enough work on the dress that I could finish it off. I used a sparkly, big earring as a brooch and that worked really well.

The jobs that the mother of the bride usually handles had been parceled out all around the circle. Everyone was pitching in. Helen, who would soon be my in-law, was around more than she might have been otherwise. That was a real bonus for me, because we got to know each other better and she was very good company. We'd work on things together. She was craft-oriented, so she had some ideas for centerpieces and the like. One day, she approached me with a different kind of project. She said, "Let's you and I write letters to our grandchildren. That way, they'll know that we thought about them and that we loved them even before they were born."

That's how she framed it, but I understood very well that that project was really for me to leave something for the grandkids I would not have the chance to know. We did it and I was glad.

Then she came to me and said, "Well, I have another idea. Why don't you and I keep journals? I got us each one and we can jot down our thoughts about the wedding."

So I started to keep the journal. Of course it's for Christine or whoever wants to read it later, but we acted like it was just for us.

We are a family of people who love to dance. So do the Quintanas. Jay and Ben's father, Ray, put on dark glasses and exited the church dancing down the aisle to "Soul Man." Later, at the reception, even my quiet, seventy-six-year-old mom got up and boogied. Late into the night, there was ballroom, salsa, and line dancing, as well as some—like the watermelon crawl and the gator—that defy description.

But the dance that meant the most to me was a slow dance with my son Jeff. As we moved in circles around the dance floor, he told me that taking care of me when I first got sick was a turning point for him. It had been, he said, the thing that had opened his eyes and changed his life. He had been feeling sort of directionless, but he told me that watching me chase my dream had inspired him to follow his dreams and never give up.

It had not been clear, when I got the third diagnosis, if I would live to see Christine married. She had offered to move up the ceremony, but I'd told her not to change the date. I made her wedding my goal. It might seem silly, but once I did that, I felt safe. I knew that I would live to dance at her wedding.

Then I couldn't die during the honeymoon, because that would ruin it for Christine, and Jeff had no intention, he said, of letting me off the hook for his graduation, so forget that. And then Christine wanted a baby right away and she refused to go through pregnancy and childbirth without me, so it looked like I was committed to life for another year.

Chapter 21
But Not Today

I'D BACKED WAY OFF INVESTIGATIVE WORK WHILE
I got into the swing of treatment. Mollie did everything and tried to carry the whole show. For about six months, she worked ten cases at one time, which was just insanity. It would have been too much for anyone. After a while, I picked up a few cases, ones that were uncomplicated, logistically and emotionally. I carefully kept a professional distance from those clients.

Mollie's and my partnership ended a few months after the wedding. Mollie went on to specialize in background searches with her own company. While the split wasn't easy, there's much about our years of working together to look back on fondly. I still miss the camaraderie of that time.

Tina opened her own PI business. Sherri, who had inherited the Grandma and Monique case, became co-owner of a PI firm, as well. Hanady had mentored them both, so I couldn't have been prouder. It was a little like seeing your kids grow up and go out into the world.

Really, I was witness to a torch being passed.

I was having tumor markers taken and having CAT scans every three or four weeks. I felt the same, whether my markers were up or down. Waiting for the results was very stressful. If I had a CAT scan and it wasn't good, they'd say, well, let's look at the tumor markers, because they're more accurate. And then when the tumor markers were up, they'd say, well, let's look at the CAT scan, because we can really see what's going on.

Then they stopped both tests while they tried a particular drug. They didn't want to be responding, they said, to the ups and downs of the markers, but to give the treatment a chance to work. At first I objected to not testing, but my oncologist pointed out that I was putting too much emphasis on the tests and it wasn't doing me any good.

In fact, I found life easier without having to anticipate results. I decided I'd assume that my treatment was working unless I heard otherwise.

By fall, I was getting infusions every week and I'd feel really bad for three or four days afterward. It was the first time treatment had made me really ill. When my doctor discontinued the chemo, I didn't want to stop, but, in fact, I did feel better without those drugs.

The disease was advancing. It was happening. We weren't out of options, but it was still tough. There were times when I'd get depressed.

Then Tia and Jeff left Twin Falls and moved in with us. That was the best thing they could have done. Before they moved in, I was spending far too much time blobbed out on the couch watching television. I didn't know there were so many court shows on TV. But with Tia there, I didn't waste time. She was always at the gym or else working one of her three jobs. That energy was contagious. With Jeff around, I was guaranteed hugs six times a day and repeated confirmations that I was the most wonderful person in the world.

After she moved in, Tia went back to Twin Falls for a few days to clean out their apartment. She called me from there, crying. I asked her if she was homesick.

She said, "Yes. I didn't think it would be like this. Twin Falls is my home."

"I know that feeling," I said, "because every time I had to move, I hated it. I hated having to leave a place I'd come to love. And then I'd come to love that new place and I wouldn't want to make that next move. It's a process."

"You are going to feel sad," I told her. "It takes a while, but you will come out the other side." I wasn't just talking about the move.

The first time I had cancer, it turned out to be an overwhelming gift. I grew as a person. I learned to appreciate my life and loved ones much more. After my treatment, every moment was many times sweeter. I was feeling better than ever. I was willing to take risks, to learn from my mistakes and to grow. I decided to finally live my dreams.

After my second diagnosis and treatment, I asked God for a break from all that learning and growing. He gave me almost four years. Then, it came back.

Cancer.

The third time, I decided to use it to my advantage. "I want to take a trip to the coast," I would say to my family. "Let's go to the coast." If they hesitated, I would bring out the big guns: *I have cancer.*

I talked to it. I gave my disease a personality. It was Fred to me. I pointed out to Fred repeatedly that it was in his interest that we coexist. If he took over, we were both done.

I fought it. I rallied my body like the captain of a team. *Go, fight, win, Rah, rah rah.* I sounded more like a determined cheerleader than a soccer mom.

I exorcised it. I would say, in a loud voice as loud as I could muster, "Begone with you Nasty Disease!" I liked that "Begone with you" part. It sounded like something an ancient disease would understand.

I prayed about it. God says that if we ask, He will answer. I just struggled with getting Him to give me the answer I wanted. That dang "all-knowing" bit was a real stumbling block. I realized that the only way around it was to accept that it was better to agree with Him, since He knew what was best.

It was just that simple.

It was just that hard.

I didn't want to die because of the people I loved, the people who loved me and would miss me. I wanted to be part of their lives. I knew that that would be the hardest part, leaving my husband and my kids behind. Time together now was extremely, intensely sweet. It was as if whole years of laughter, sorrow, joy—everything—were compressed into a smaller time frame.

As I faced the end, I thought back over my life, my own retrospective of sorts.

I had turned a death sentence into a whole new life. I made being middle-aged and overlooked into a magic cloak. I had vaulted over the barrier of my own shyness; I stepped up to knock on doors, becoming whoever I wanted to be. I had pulled Dad close, and in his last days, that was an amazing, wonderful gift to us both. I worked with fabulous women—Jan, Mollie, Tina, and many more. I had shown my children what it is to pursue a dream and never give up. I helped some people. I saw lives that were tragic, especially children's lives, and that was sad, but a lot of the time, we had fun.

We had the most fun. So much fun.

People always asked me if I was afraid on the job. The answer was no, because I had faced true danger every hour of every day. I knew, firsthand, what it was to struggle for life. Because of that, I lost my fear. I learned to tear off the wig. I focused on the essential thing, that one thing I could do that made me feel good about myself, and I found that I was able to do it.

I wasn't the perfect candidate to become an investigator. I was a soccer mom in a minivan. I had no law-enforcement background and I wasn't particularly observant. But I wanted to make it happen, so I still became a successful PI.

I didn't realize every dream. I wasn't crowned Miss America. I never became a singer or a cheerleader. I didn't walk a tightrope.

But I did become a Spymom.

I did accomplish that.

Afterword

AS I SIT, TRYING TO FIND THE WORDS TO WRITE, I keep thinking about what my mom would do. *What would she say and what would she want me to say?* If I didn't keep this section upbeat, lively, witty, and a little bit sentimental, I wouldn't be doing her justice.

My mother was my best friend. We could confide in each other. She was the first person I would call to share something funny, to pass along gossip, to cry, or to celebrate. We had a set lunch date every week. She would update me on all of her cases. I was always fascinated by the things she got into and she was an excellent storyteller (her sister Jan has this same talent). I loved to hear about her cases and her world. Not every person gets to tell people that their mom is a famous private investigator.

One of the things my mom always said to me was, "Dance, little girl, dance!" I don't think we ever wrote a note or card to each other that didn't contain some version of that quote. She believed that a central point of living is to fully enjoy the moment—get out on the floor, have fun, and dance!

Never was this passion for life more evident to me than on my wedding day. Even with a body riddled with cancer, she never let the disease dampen her spirit or keep her from having the time of her life. It is hard to describe how radiant she looked as she mingled with family and friends, delivered a heartfelt and hilarious toast, and let loose on the dance floor. I will always remember her just like she was that night, making the most of every moment.

Shortly after the wedding, she took a turn for the worse. After a decade of battling cancer, the relentless disease eventually spread too much to contain and her body couldn't fight anymore. On March 14, 2009, my mother, Valerie Ann Agosta, passed away.

The last couple of months were very difficult for her and for our entire family. She was completely exhausted, but she worked hard to finish the last parts of the book. Wearing a cute knitted cap on her head, with her makeup bag within arm's length, she would spend days on end writing and editing. My mother was creative and had a natural way with words. She had always wanted to be a writer and this book was her dream. The hope of seeing it published helped keep her alive and gave her a goal to work toward. We would talk about the release of the book and I almost convinced her that she'd be here to see it happen. But I think we both knew the sad truth.

If there was an award for the most memorable hospital patient, I'm sure my mom would have won that prize hands down. She was so charming, hospitable, and hilarious during her final days. Some of the things she said still make me smile to this day. I often wonder if she did that intentionally so that when those memories came back to me, I would always find something to smile about in the midst of my tears.

My family felt a strange mix of unbelievable sadness and relief after she passed. Although we had acknowledged that she would most likely not ultimately beat this disease, there was a piece of me that hadn't believed that this vibrant, beautiful, brave woman couldn't overcome anything. She seemed almost invincible.

My mom always knew how to get what she wanted and she had requested specific things for her funeral. She was always the party planner and already had photos that she wanted me to display, as well as songs for her tribute video. She wanted her funeral to be a celebration of her life!

It was amazing how many people showed up. The entire church (upstairs and downstairs) was crowded with family, friends, neighbors, and clients. There were many people whom I had never before met, all of whom had stories to tell about my mother. It was great to meet people who had spent time with her and knew her in different ways. Some were old friends from out of state; others knew her for only a brief time. But it seemed that she had made an everlasting impression on all of them.

We waited until Mother's Day to spread her ashes. We thought that would allow us to celebrate her on a day that was going to be difficult for us. The location was perfect: a beautiful pond with a fountain, surrounded by colorful flowers and shade trees, adjacent to a trail we often hiked with Kasey. There is a sandy beach in front of the pond, which is where each one of us took turns saying our favorite thing about our mother. We dispersed her ashes there on the sand and spread them around with our bare feet. We saved a small portion to spread at her father's marker, which is on a nearby hill overlooking her site. It was an amazing way to leave a part of her with her father, who was a huge part of her life.

Afterward, as part of my mom's request, we released bright colored helium balloons with personal notes attached to send up to her. It was beautiful to see all the balloons cascading to the sky, just like she knew it would. We stood there watching until they were so high, they flew out of sight. I had tears in my eyes but a smile on my face as I watched my balloon, which had a simple but perfect message: "Mom, I'll always miss you, and never forget to 'Dance, little girl, dance!"

Since her death, we have all tried to live our lives in a way that would make her proud. We know she would have wanted us to turn this difficult situation into something positive.

My dad has recently retired from his job and is trying to get back to a normal life. He is doing really well and is currently trying to decide what he wants to be when he grows up. Thanks to my mom, he's realized that it's never too late to chase your dreams. I know that whatever he decides to do, he'll be great at it.

Jeff was always interested in filmmaking, so he recently premiered an independent film that he wrote, directed, and produced, and dedicated it to our mother. I was so proud of him, and my mom would have been jumping up and down with excitement. It was a huge success and a great start to a film career. But I could see it in Jeff's eyes that the one thing missing was our mom.

Scott is the baby of the family. It breaks my heart when I think that he was only twenty-one when our mother died. He is intelligent, caring, and fun. I know my mom would have wanted to see him graduate from college, get married, and have children. We know he'll do all of these things and more.

As for me, I don't even know where to begin. I've always loved it when people told me that I remind them so much of my mom. Now I treasure those words more than ever. They're just another way that I can feel connected to her even though she is not here with me.

She was my confidante, best friend, adviser, comedian, and shopping buddy. She chased her dreams and had an amazing career doing what she loved, but she was also, first and foremost, a wonderful person and mother. We had the most exciting Christmases, birthdays, family game nights—so many traditions that we'll always keep.

The hardest part for us is knowing that she'll never meet her grandchildren. However, they will know about her through our traditions and through her words. Although she isn't here to see her book in print, physically here to touch it, I know she's somewhere out there cheering it on.

—Christine Agosta Quintana

September 2009

In Loving Memory
Jay, Christine, Jeff, Scott, Ben, and Tia